T0135917

Thammasat University
Faculty of Science and Technology
Department of Computer Science
Bangkok, Thailand

Beuth-Hochschule für Technik
University of Applied Sciences
Department for Informatics & Media
Berlin, Germany

# Proceedings of Software Engineering and Quality Assurance
# Technical Report #1

Roland Petrasch, Songsak Rongviriyapanich (Eds.)

Bibliographic information published by the Deutsche Nationalbibliothek

The Deutsche Nationalbibliothek lists this publication in the Deutsche
Nationalbibliografie; detailed bibliographic data are available
in the Internet at http://dnb.d-nb.de .

ISBN 978-3-8325-3399-1

Logos Verlag Berlin GmbH
Comeniushof, Gubener Str. 47,
10243 Berlin
Tel.: +49 (0)30 42 85 10 90
Fax: +49 (0)30 42 85 10 92
INTERNET: http://www.logos-verlag.de

# Editorial

This first technical report contains the results of joint activities in the context of the cooperation between the Thammasat University, Department of Computer Science, Faculty of Science and Technology, Rangsit Campus (Bangkok, Thailand) and the Beuth Hochschule für Technik, University of Applied Sciences, Department for Informatics and Media (Berlin, Germany).

The main focus is on software engineering, IT project management and quality assurance. We want to give our academic staff, students and research partners a platform in order to present their work to the public. This report contains several excerpts from thesis work of Thai and German students. It also presents some preparation work necessary for the joint research project AMDIS started in 2011. The AMDIS project aims to provide an infrastructure for agile model-driven development of interactive systems. An example for an essential component for such an infrastructure are HCI (Human Computer Interaction) Patterns (or Usability Patterns). The next technical report (planned for 2013) will describe the outcomes of the project in detail.

Together we want to contribute to a professional and international software engineering education. There must be a way out of "Software's Chronic Crisis" (W. Wayt Gibbs). The time of software that crash, users who lose data or cannot finish their work must belong to the past. Our lecturers, research staff and students help to build better, i.e. usable software system.


Songsak Rongviriyapanich, Roland Petrasch


November 2012, Bangkok and Berlin

# Table of Contents

# Extending Platform Independent Models with Security Features

Nattakan Suppajak, Songsakdi Rongviriyapanish

Computer Science Department
Faculty of Science and Technology
Thammasat University, Bangkok, Thailand

## Abstract

The Model-Driven Architecture (MDA) concept is a recent evolution of software development that uses models to drive software processes. MDA provides different levels of models. A Platform Independent Model (PIM) is a model that represents application details but no specific platform details. PIMs are usually represented in UML. Developing applications in a conventional way, analyst and designer will concentrate first on the functional requirements to create PIM. While the non-functional requirements, especially security, will be incorporated after completing the application development. This leads to greatly increased development costs when defects are found.

In practice, conventional application development projects often have difficulties in managing non-functional requirements during the early project phases: Analysts and designers concentrate mainly on functional requirements in order to create PIMs. Non-functional requirements, especially security, are specified informally or vague, leaving a semantic gap between analysis and design. This leads to increasingly error prone solutions or at least the risk remains high that the requirements are not fulfilled properly. Also error correction in the late phases or after deployment is much more expensive than in early phases.

In this paper, we propose an approach to extending PIMs with security features early in analysis and design phases. The security requirements cover authentication, confidentiality and integrity. Security features are extended to the UML metamodel. This approach will help analysts and designers who are not security experts to correctly incorporate security requirement to PIM. We also propose an approach to transforming PIM with security features to Platform Specific Model (PSM). We used a web application with web services and Java Server Pages (Servlet) as an example to validate our approach. WS-Security and Servlet's security specification are used for implementing security requirements.

# 1. Introduction

The Model-Driven Architecture (MDA) [1] concept uses a model-centric perspective to drive software development processes. In analysis and design phase, the system analyst and designer will create a PIM (Platform Independent Model) to describe the functionality of an application. A PIM contains no details of technological platforms. PIMs that are represented in UML (Unified Modeling Language) contain only functional requirements while non-functional requirements are often not included.

In many application development processes in practice, software developers concentrate primarily on the creation of application models based on functional requirements while non-functional requirement, especially security, are considered during or after the implementation phase. This leads to increased development efforts when the defects are found [2]. Moreover, most application analysts (and developers) are not security experts, therefore security requirements are poorly specified and implemented. In order to design an application with security requirements a security expert is requires during the whole project. This increases the development cost significantly. Therefore, many researches propose approaches that take account of non-functional requirement such as reliability, performance [8], and security [4, 5, and 6] during the analysis and design phase so that defects can be avoided and cost of development can be reduced. In other words, considering non-functional requirements in the analysis and design phase contributes to improved productivity and maintainability.

In this paper, we propose an approach to extending PIM with security features which help analysts to add the security requirements into PIM in analysis and design phase. Furthermore, we propose an approach to transforming PIM with security properties to Platform Specific Model (PSM) which implements the security properties too. To validate our approach, we apply it to develop a web service application and use WS-Security to realize security requirements since WS-Security provides the solution to implementing authentication, confidentiality, and integrity [3]. Moreover, these platforms are mature and widely used.

The rest of this paper is organized as follows: Section 2 presents background and related works. Section 3 describes the proposed approach to extending the security features to PIM metamodel. Section 4 describes case study and the way to apply our approach. Finally, In Section 5 we conclude our work.

## 2. Background and Related Work

In this section, we discuss the existing works of the approaches to integrating security requirement to the application model. Jan Jurjens [4] proposed UMLsec, which allows expressing relevant security information within the diagram in a system specification. The approach is specific on Multi-Level Security such as secure network link. This research concentrates on design level, but does not show transformation concept. We bring the concept of adding security in design model in our work, but we concentrate on different kind of security requirement.

Torsten Lodderstedt et al. [5] proposed SecureUML, is an approach similar to UMLsec but they focused on designing security model based on Role-Based Access Control (RBAC) concept. They provided an example of generating EJB application to validate their concepts. In our research, we use their concepts of implementation in MDA context. Contrast to our work, their approach does not cover other security requirements such as integrity and confidentiality.

Yuichi Nakamura et al. [6] proposed a tooling framework to generate web service security configurations using MDA approach. Their approach generated a security configuration files and binding for Websphere Application Server. It differs from our approach: Yuichi Nakamura et al. concentrate on transformation on a model-to-code level while our approach covers both levels, model-to-model and model-to-code. For the security concern in their work they used WS-Security standard too, but only for marking the application model. They do not create a metamodel or an UML profile for web service security.

## 3. Our Approach

In our research, we focus on how to extend the security requirement to PIM and transform PIMs to PSMs. An approach starts by letting the analysts and designers analyze the security requirements and suitably select a security element from a defined set of security elements that we propose and add selected security elements to PIM. Then, we transform PIM with added security elements ito PSMs by using a set of transformation rules we define. Finally, we generate source codes and configuration files from the PSM with security property.

We implement a case study application to prove our proposed PIM metamodel that we extended with security features. We choose two platforms, Java web service and Servlet, for implementing our case study application. Analyst and designer can use our PIM metamodel with security features to create PIM of application. Furthermore, we propose PSMs metamodel and set of transformation rules for transforming PIM to PSMs. Finally, after generating source code and configuration file from the PSMs with security features, the implementer can use the generated code to complete the application. An overview of our approach is shown in Figure 1.

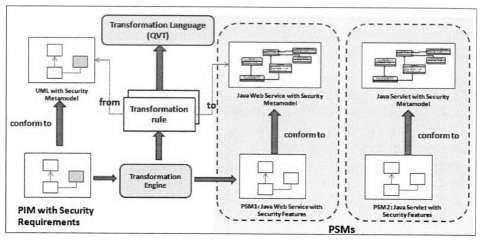

Figure 1. an overview of our approach

## 3.1. Security Features

Security Requirement is one of the most important non-functional requirement. Most of the e-commerce applications require security to protect them from attacker and other threats. From that reason, capturing the security requirement of system is a hard task that must be handled at the early stage of system development [13]. For solving this problem, we propose to extend PIM metamodel with security features which helps analyst add security requirement in the first step of development process.

In the research, the security requirements we are interested in are authentication, confidentiality and integrity since they are the basic securities usually used in many type of applications such as web application or web service. The definition of each security requirement is given below. [14]

- Authentication: "The granting of access rights to a user, program, or process"

- Confidentiality: "The concept of holding sensitive data in confidence, limited to an appropriate set of individuals or organizations"

8

- Integrity: "The property that data meet an a priori expectation of quality."

## 3.2. Extending PIM metamodel with Security Features

In development process, analyst and designer usually describe system requirement (both functional and non-functional requirement) in UML. In this research, we present the security requirement using class diagram, which shows the static view. We add security features into PIM metamodel by extending UML metamodel. The benefit of this approach is that we can define a language to describe a PIM more meaningful than describing with UML profile. The structure of UML metamodel used in this research is basically structured following to [17],[18]. In the next section we describe how to add security features to PIM metamodel.

We use the concept of OOAD (Object-Oriented Analysis and Design) [15] to analyze the security definitions to design the security features in PIM metamodel. The process of analysis security features is described as follows:

1. Collect the definition of security features from different sources (We collect the definition from [14][21][22][23][24]).

2. Categorize the definition by the type of security, authentication, confidentiality and integrity. Delete the definition that not related to the three security types.

3. Analyze and design security metamodel using OOAD steps as follows:

   - Finding class and attribute.

   - Finding association.

   - Create classes and their relationships.

Then we bring classes and relationships to extend PIM metamodel. After extending we have finally PIM metamodel as shown in Figure 2.

The structure of our extended PIM metamodel contains two parts; the first one consists of the classes of UML metamodel (in yellow and orange), the second one consists of the new classes representing security features (in purple). We define a class named SecurityRequirement which represents a security feature. It can be inherited in three types of security requirement such as Authentication, Confidentiality and Integrity. Analyst and designer can specify security features in PIM by using attribute secreqs into Class, Attribute and Operation elements.

The structure of Authentication in PIM metamodel will verify user to access system by UserIdentity element. This element use to define user that will have right way to access resource. There are four classes extending it such as Credential, SmartCard, AuthenticationServer and PublicKey.

The structure of Confidentiality contains AuthorizedParty and Action elements. Confidentiality has meaning to hiding data or information from unauthorized party to do some Action such as Reading, Listening, Recording or Removing. The AuthorizedParty has three types; Individual, Organization and Proceses.

The main meaning of integrity is nobody can not modified data or information. In PIM metamodel, we define integrity requirement by using Integrity element. We use AuthorizedParty represent the user that have right to modified data. The data in this case it mean class, attribute or operation. We already explain set of AuthorizeParty in last section.

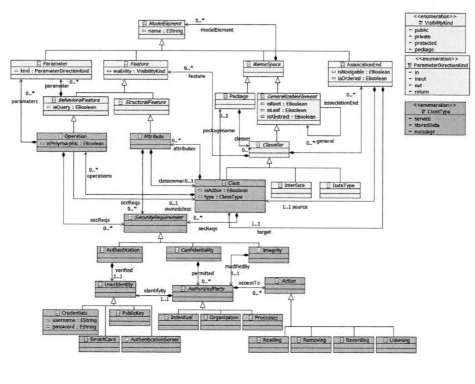

UML (Basic)　　UML (Extended )　　Security Element

Figure 2. PIM metamodel with security property

Furthermore, we extend ClassType; property of Class element, for describe special type of Class. By using service for describe this Class can call from other, using storedData for describe this Class can be persist in some way.

In analysis and design phase, analyst and designer can create PIM that conform to PIM metamodel. In this step, they have PIM that represent functional requirement of application and this PIM already has security requirement too.

## 3.3. PSM metamodel

In order to prove that we can create a real application that has security property with our extended PIM metamodel with security features, we must be able to create a PIM of a case study application and implement it with at least two different PSMs. In our research, we choose two platforms, Java web service and Java Servlet, as PSMs because the implementation for the security on these platforms are based on a very clear specification. Servlet is a web component in J2EE container and has security management based on specification of J2EE [16]. While WS-Security [9], [10] (defined by OMG) is a security specification which can be applied for Java web service.

In our research, we implement Java web service application using Apache Axis framework [11] and using Apache Rampart [12] to manage security on web service. The J2EE architecture as shown in Figure 3. For implementing Servlet application, the security management defined by Servlet specification contains authentication, confidentiality, integrity and access control. While WS-Security defines two levels of security 1) transportation level and 2) message level. In this research, we use the message level because it comprises three security features we focus, authentication, integrity and confidentiality. The Apache Rampart framework also implements this standard.

In designing metamodel step, we do not add the detail of framework because we want to define them in common. In addition, the designed PSM can be implemented with any framework that it represents the re-usability of software development and make the development process more efficient.

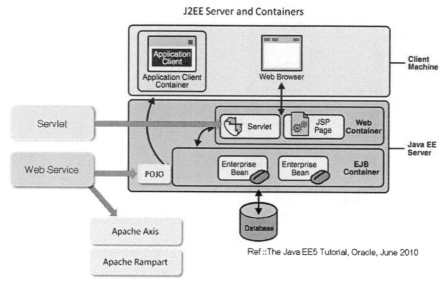

Figure 3. J2EE Architecture

## 3.3.1 Design PSM of Java Web Service with WS-Security

We define PSM of Java web service metamodel by using Java metamodel standard defined by OMG [19] as base and extend a part of web service security by using WS-Security specification[10]. We use the same approach described in 3.2.1 to extend Java metamodel with security elements except that we use XML schema of WS-Security as input to analyze. The metamodel of java web service with security features is shown in Figure 4.

Basically the implementation of java web service is defined as a method of Java class. Therefore, the mechanism to specify the security of a web service is to define the security property at the method level. Analyst can use the Protection element in our extended web service metamodel to specify one of the security features, Authentication, Confidentiality or Integrity, required for a web service.

The authentication property is represented by Authentication element. Following to WS-Security specification, we can use UsernameToken [20] to manage authentication. We define the structure of UsernameToken comprising username, password and other property: Nonce and Created used to identify who can access to this service.

The specification in WS-Security specifies the implementation of confidentiality by XML encryption. We extend the confidentiality part in metamodel with the EncryptedKey element which specifies the mechanism of encryption.

Finally, to guarantee the integrity we use the mechanism of XML signature. The structure of signature contains CanonicalizationMethod element for defining a method to sign and KeyInfo element for defining a key to use in signing process.

## 3.3.2 Design PSM of Servlet with Security

Servlets are web components in Java Enterprise Edition (J2EE) Architecture which we use to implement web application in our case study. From the specification of J2EE [16], we can implement security part for Servlet application by specifying security elements in its deployment descriptor or web.xml.

Therefore, we can define security metamodel of Servlet by following the structure of security elements which defined in J2EE specification. In this research, we use the specification of Servlet version 2.4. We extend the security features to metamodel of Servlet at the Class level since a Servlet is defined by class. We define Protection element represent the security features. All of these three security requirements which are authentication, confidentiality, and integrity are provided the security attributes by using this element. The identification feature is defined by LoginConfig which can be customized to define the identification scenario. For example, we can define the identification mechanism whether basic http security or developing the program to check the authentication of user. In cases of confidentiality and integrity, we can enable these feature by SecurityConstraint element. Using SecurityConstraint element, we can define the type of TransportGuarantee for both of Confidentiality and Integrity via customize the element to CONFIDENTIAL and INTEGRAL respectively.

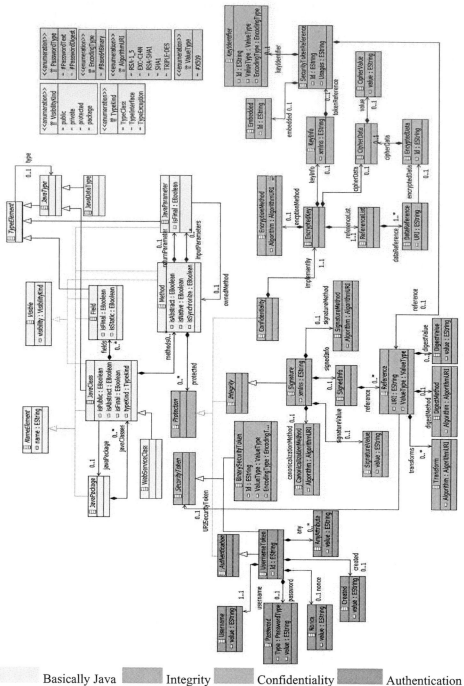

Basically Java     Integrity     Confidentiality     Authentication

Figure. 4 web service metamodel extended with security features

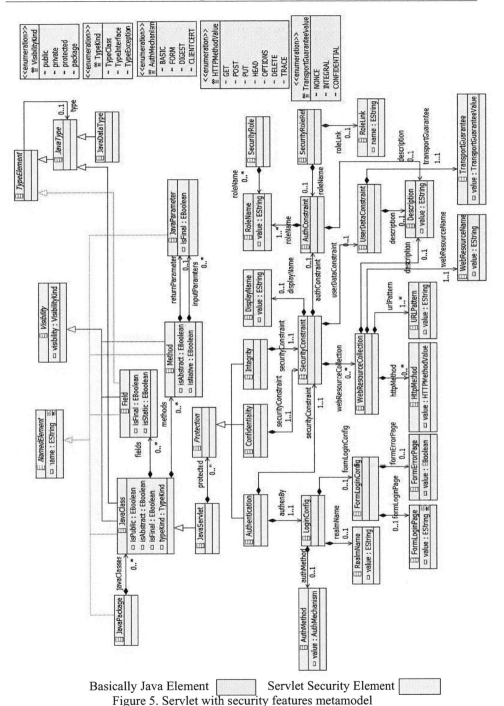

Basically Java Element ☐☐☐☐  Servlet Security Element ☐☐☐☐

Figure 5. Servlet with security features metamodel

## 3.4. Model Transformation

In transformation process, we use model-to-model transformations. In this approach, both source and target models are conform to their metamodel. The PIM with security property must conform to PIM with security metamodel (explained in 3.1.1). The target models are Java web service and Servlet with security property. PSMs are automatically generated and must conform to their metamodel. After the transformation the PSM elements contain security properties.

Transformation rules and the transformation engine are important parts in the model transformation process. The transformation rules are mappings between PIM metamodel and PSM metamodel elements. We use Query / View / Transformation (QVT) [7] language to define transformation rules. QVT is standard language defined by OMG. It contains sub-languages; QVT Relations, QVT Operational Mapping and Core. We used the declarative language QVT Relations.

In this section, we present an example of transformation rules for transforming Class elements in PIM with Authentication elements to Java Servlet Class with Authentication property. Then, we define a mapping between PIM metamodel and Java Servlet metamodel elements before we define the transformation rules. Defining a mapping makes a definition of transformation rules easier. The mapping between PIM metamodel and Servlet metamodel for authentication property can separate in three cases depending on the value of UserIdentity. If we choose UserIdentity by Credentials, our rule generates a Java Servlet Class using BASIC mechanism to do authentication process. We define this rule named `ClassToJavaServletAuthC`. If we choose UserIdentity by PublicKey, rule generates Java Servlet Class using CLIENT-CERT mechanism. We define this rule named `ClassToJavaServletAuthPK`. Finally, if we choose UserIdentity by AuthenticationServer, rule generates Java Servlet Class using FORM mechanism. This rule is named `ClassToJava ServletAuthServer`. The mapping that we explained is shown in Figure 6.

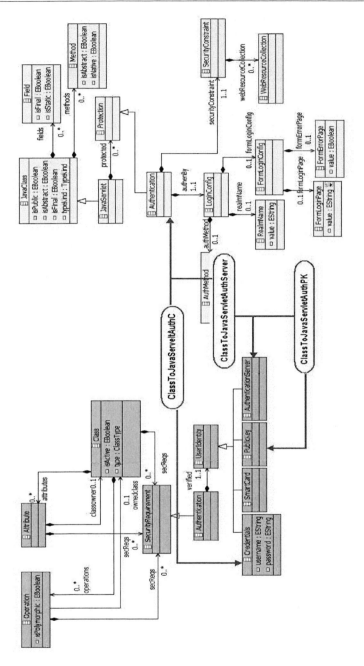

Figure 6. mapping between PIM metamodel and Servlet metamodel for authentication property

Then, we define transformation rule for each of three mapping cases. We show an example of transformation rule named `ClassToJavaServlet AuthC`. This rule transforms a Class which requires an authentication to verify Credentials to generate a Servlet Class which uses BASIC authentication mechanism to checking user credential. The BASIC authentication mechanism in Servlet security uses default mechanism of HTTP protocol to verify user credential. It automatically generates a login form when user sends a request to the Servlet which required an authentication. In transformation process, this rule will validate any classes in PIM that has the ClassType service and that has an authentication security requirement which has UserIdentity in Credentials. If this condition is true, it generates a Servlet class which has authentication property in BASIC mechanism. This rule as shown in Figure 7.

```
relation ClassToJavaServletAuthC {
        cn, uname, pass : String;
        isAbstract : Boolean;

checkonly domain umlsec c:umlsec::Class{
        name = cn,
        isAbstract = isAbstract,
        type = umlsec::ClassType::service,
        secreqs = rq:umlsec::Authentication{
        verified = user : umlsec::Credentials {
          username = uname,
          password = pass
        }
        }
};

enforce domain jssec jc:javaserv::JavaServlet {
        name = cn,
        isAbstract = isAbstract,
        typeKind = javaserv::TypeKind::TypeClass,
        protected = prot:javaserv::Authentication{
        loginConfig = l:javaserv::LoginConfig{
          authMethod = auth:javaserv::AuthMethod{
            value = javaserv::
                AuthMechanism::BASIC
          },
          realmName = r:javaserv::RealmName{
            value = 'Default'
            }
        },
....
```

Figure 7. rule for transforming Class to java Servlet Class (authentication property)

Furthermore, we can define the transformation rules for transforming PIM to Java Web Service in the same way.

# 4. Case Study

To prove our approach that it can implement a real application, we present the implementation of case study. In the implementation of our case study we show the whole life cycle of development process. In this research, we mainly use Eclipse Modeling Framework (EMF) to create metamodel and PIM and use mediniQVT for defining the transformation rules from PIM to PSM. In model-to-code transformation step, we used Acceleo (Eclipse plug-in) to generate source code and configuration files.

## 4.1. Use Cases

In this section, we describe the system requirements of our case study which is an e-commerce application, called One-Stop Services. It is a project of Software Industry Promotion Agency (Public Organization) whose objective is to provide service for Thai people to pay electric bill online.

This project contains two subsystems; the first one is the electric online payment system and the second one is the PEA system that is a back office system for the Provincial Electricity Authority. PEA provides meter information and meter registration services. The electric online payment system is a public web application for paying electric bills online. This system uses some services from the PEA system. In term of a SOA architecture, we call the PEA system a service provider and the electric online payment system a service requester.

This project has some sensitive data such as payment transaction and personal data. Therefore, non-functional requirement especially security are very importance. Then, the communication between these subsystems must be secured too.

The online payment system consists of 5 use cases:

- Register to Member : User register to member of system.
- Login :  Using for validate member.
- Register Meter : User register electric meter number.
- Cancel Meter : User cancel electric meter.
- Pay Electric Bill : User can pay electric bill.

The PEA system has 3 use cases:

- Validate Meter Owner: Using for validate the meter owner.

- Request Bill Information: providing the bill information.

- Update Bill Status: To update payment status.

The "Register to Member" and "Register Meter" use cases are communicate with all use cases of PEA system. Then, all use case of PEA System and two use cases of electric online payment system must be apply security requirements.

In register to member use case must call validate meter owner use case to validating this user is a meter owner or not. And when we call validate meter owner use case must user that have authorize to call it. The request bill information use case is called by the pay electric bill use case. In this case, bill information is sensitive data then it want to hide this data from unauthorized party to reading them. Finally, user pay electric bill and in this use case call update bill status use case. If payment process is finished, we want to update payment status. In this use case, payment data contains payment code and amount, which they are sensitive data. Therefore, the data in this step must have integrity property; do not be modified in any case. From these requirements the analyst can create PIM that shown in next section.

## 4.2. PIM and PSM

In this section, we present the detail of PIM and PSM of case study. In this step, the analyst capture functional and non-functional requirements of system. Then, they create PIM which represent both functional and security requirements. This PIM as shown in Figure 8. PIM of PEA system contains four classes; PeaUser, Meter, Billing and Payment.

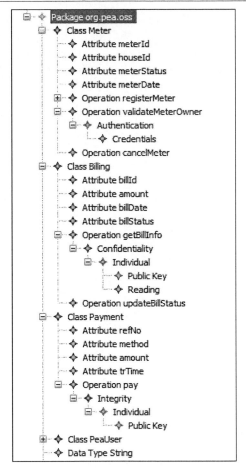

Figure 8. PIM of PEA system

The PeaUser class represents the meter owner with user data such as user-code, name, personalID and address. The Meter class represents the electric meter, has meter properties such as meterId and houseId and it has a `valid-ateMeterOwner` operation. And they set authentication property on this operation and define the identity of user by a Credential. The Billing class has properties such as billId, amount and billDate and has `getBillInfo` operation. This operation provides bill information for requester, bill data which return to requester must be a confidential data. Therefore, they add Confidentiality to this method and set Reading action and defined UserIdentity in Public Key. Finally, Payment class which used for manages data of payment and has operation pay to providing bill payment for user. They add Integrity property to this operation which wants to have integrity data.

21

If they already create the PIM, they bring this PIM to model transformation process. The transformation process will automated generate PSM by using set of relations which define in section 3.4. The PSM contains four classes; one java class and three web service classes. The Billing class in PIM will be generated to Billing web service class in PSM. This class has getBillInfo method which has confidentiality property. The detail of confidentiality property contains EncryptedKey, KeyInfo and encryption method. The PSM in java web service of PEA system as shown in Figure 9.

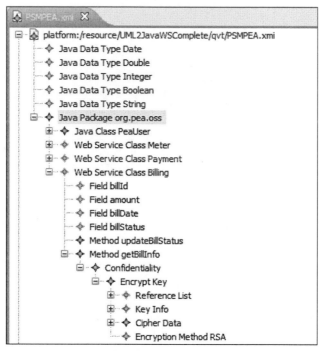

Figure 9. PSM in web service platform

In this part, we present an approach to create application in Java Servlet platform. We use same system requirement from PEA system. The PIM of Servlet application as shown in Figure 10. In this PIM, they add the security requirement in class level because in the Servlet's security management that manages in class level.

In addition, the structure of PIM be analysis from functional and security requirement which the same as the PIM that create for web service application development. The Meter class has authentication property, The Billing class has Confidentiality property and the Payment class has integrity property. In this section, we will show the authentication property in PIM. The authentication property can add to class in PIM in 3 cases; difference by type of UserIdentity. If UserIdentity is Credentials, it generate PSM which has verification type is required username and password.

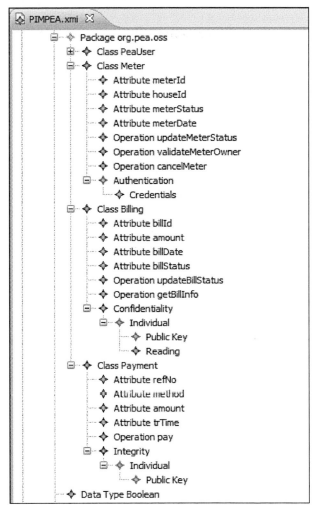

Figure 10. PIM for develop Servlet application

Then, they bring the PIM in Figure 10 into transformation process. The PSM of Servlet application with authentication property that shown in Figure 11. The Meter class with authentication property and has Credential can be generated to JavaServlet class with has authentication property too. An authentication property in PSM that is described in BASIC authentication method. The other part contains security constraints which represent resource's name,

HTTP method and URL pattern. The designer can change or update authentication property that you want such as want to add more HTTP mechanism; PUT or DELETE.

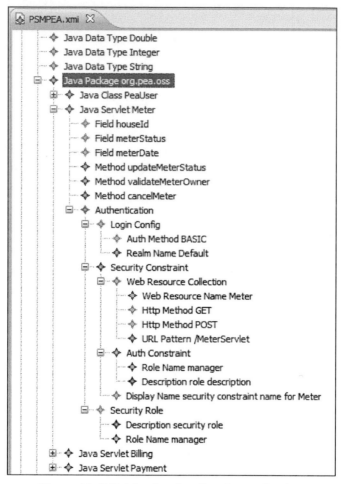

Figure 11. PSM for develop Servlet application

In this step, we already have the PSM of web service application and the PSM of Servlet application. Then, we want to bring PSMs to generate source code and configuration files which particular to platform. The transformation in this step call model-to-code. We use the tool "Acceleo" (OMG MOFM2T implementation) which is an Eclipse plug-in to create the templates for generate source code and configuration files.

In model-to-code transformation step, we must define the template for generate code first. For java web service application, we define template of web service class and template of web service configuration files. To develop web service application we use Apache Axis framework and use Apache Rampart module to manage security property. Then, the configuration files must have structure follow by Rampart's specification. In Figure 13, folder output is contained artifacts which are generated from transformation process. The java-classes folder contains java class and web service classes. The ws-config folder contains web service configuration files and classes that use to manage security property. We separate the configuration files in two types; for service requester side and service provider side. For web service provider development, we will bring service classes and service configuration files to pack in .aar file. (This file is based on axis framework.)

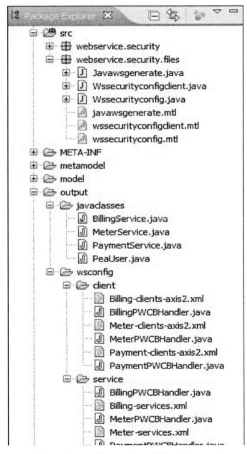

Figure 12. source code and configuration files for web service application

For the Servlet application implementation, the approach for generate code and deployment descriptor are the same concept as web service application. Then, we shortly describe transformation process and the artifacts. In this step, we create two templates; for generate Servlet class and for generate web.xml. If the transformation process finished, the security properties are defined in web.xml. After that, we will bring Servlet classes in classes folder and web.xml in folder servlet-config to pack into web application package (.war).

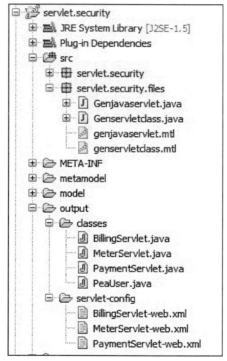

Figure 13. source code and deployment descriptor of Servlet application

## 4.3. Deploy and Testing

In deployment phase, we bring the artifacts from section 4.2 to deploy on web server such as Apache Tomcat or others J2EE server. For web service application, after deploy web service application on Apache Axis, the service can show in Figure 14. The BillingService has getBillingInfo operation which has confidentiality property. If any requester want to send request to call this operation, this request must comply in confidentiality way of Apache Rampart. To testing the security part of this service we create client to call operation getBillingInfo, the message of request and response that return from service will be encrypt. Therefore, they can guarantee that this web service application already has confidentiality property.

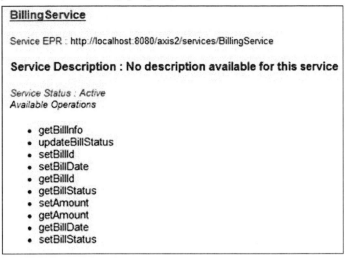

Figure 14. BillingService on Apache Axis

Figure 15. authentication login form of Java Servlet application

For Servlet application deployment, we bring the .war file which describe in section 4.2 to deploy in Apache Tomcat. Then, we can test the authentication property of Servlet application by call Meter Servlet. After we send request to MeterServlet URL, the server send login form back to user. The login form requires username and password. If user fill the username and password and send it back to server. The server will verified user identity and if it success that will do in MeterServlet logic but if it incorrect user it could not access MeterServlet. Furthermore, the confidentiality and integrity property can be testing in the same way. The login form as shown in Figure 15.

The development of case study in two different platform applications, we found that, both web service application and java Servlet application can use our approach and our extended PIM metamodel with security features to create real applications that have security property.

# 5. Conclusion

This research propose the guideline which describes the methodology to add the non-functional requirement especially security in the analysis and design phase. In this approach, we can use the extended PIM metamodel that manipulated with confidentiality, authentication, and integrity to applying the practical software development process. Especially, in analysis and design phase, this approach help the analyst and designer develop PIM with security features more easy than the traditional method. So, this way also help both of novice analyst and novice designer to evaluating the functional requirement with the security feature at the begin time of software development process as well.

In addition, the tooling which we propose in this research can apply to the software industry. The developer can use our tools to develop the software components such as java web service, java Servlet and basic java class which already have security property. These component can bring to use in the real application.

# References

[1]  J.Miller and J. Mukerji, "MDA Guide Version 1.0," OMG, 1 May 2003.

[2]  P.T. Devanbu and S.Stubbleine, "Softwate Engineering for Security: a Roadmap," ICSE 2000, vol. Future of Software Engineering.

[3]  M. Endrei, J. Ang, A. Arsanjani, S. Chua, P. Comte, P. Krogdahl, M. Luo and T. Newling, Patterns: Service-Oriented Architecture and Web Services, IBM, pp. 145-153, Apil 2004.

[4]  J.Jurjens, "UMLsec:Extending UML for Secure Systems Development," Proceedings of the 5th Conference on the Unified Modeling Language, Dresden, Germany, 2002

[5]  T. Lodderstedt, D. Basin, and J. Dorser, "SecureUML: A UML-Based Modeling Language for Model-Driven Security," Proceedings of the 5th Conference on the Unified Modeling Language, Dresden, Germany, 2002

[6]  Y. Nakamura, M. Tatsubori, T. Imamura, and K. Ono, "Model-Driven Security Based on a Web Services Security Architecture," Proceeding of the 2005 IEEE International Conference on Services Computing (SCC'05), 2005

[7]  MOF QVT Final Adopted Specification. OMG, document ad/2005-07-01

[8]  V. Cortellessa, A. D. Marco, and P. Inverardi, "Integrating Performance and Reliability Analysis in a Non-Functional MDA Framework," M.B. Dwyer and A. Lopes (Eds.): FASE 2007, LNCS 4422, pp. 57-71, 2007

[9]  N. Chase, "Understanding Web Services specifications, Part 4: WS-Security," IBM, 22 Aug 2006

[10] A. Nadalin, C. Kaler , P. Hallam-Baker and R. Monzillo, "Web Services Security: SOAP Message Security 1.0 (WS-Security 2004)" OASIS Standard 200401, March 2004"

[11] http://ws.apache.org/axis/

[12] http://ws.apache.org/rampart/

[13] NCSC-TG-004 (1988) (National Computer Security Center, USA): Glossary of Computer Security Terms. Retrieved August 19, 2010 from http://www.marcorsyscom.usmc.mil/sites/ia/references/national/ NCSC-TG-004% 20Glossary.html.

[14] A. Rodriguez , E. Fernandez-Medina, & M. Piattini (2006). Towards a UML 2.0 for the Modeling of Security Requirements in Business Processes. LNCS 4084 (pp: 51-61)

[15] I. Jacobson, & G. Booch, & J. Rumbaugh, Unified Software Development Process. India: Addison-Wesley

[16] The Java EE 5 Tutorial, Oracle (pp. 856)

29

[17] J. B´ezivin , S. Hammoudi, D. Lopes & F. Jouault. Applying MDA Approach for Web Service Platform. Proceeding of the 8th IEEE Intl Enterprise Distributed Object Computing Conf (EDOC 2004)

[18] H.Q. Nguyen. Analysis of Crosscutting Concerns in QVT-based Model Transformations. Unpublished master's thesis, University of Twente, Faculty of Mathematics and Computer Science

[19] Metamodel and UML Profile for Java and EJB Specification. OMG, document formal/04-02-02

[20] Web Services Security UsernameToken Profile 1.1. OASIS Standard Specification (2006, February).

[21] P. C. Pfleeger, & L. S. Pfleeger. Security in Computing. United States: Prentice Hall, 2006

[22] ISO/IEC 17799 (2005) Information technology–Security techniques–Code of practice for information security management. Retrieved August 19, 2010 from http://www.iso.org/iso/en/prodsservices/popstds/informationsecurity.html.

[23] Hitachi ID Systems, Inc.: Definition of Authentication. http://mtechit.com/concepts/authentication.html

[24] M. Menzel, I. Thomas, & C. Meinel. Security Requirements Specification in Service-oriented Business Process Management. 2009 International Conference on Availability, Reliability and Security, IEEE Computer Society Press

# Development of a General Rule-Set for Human Computer Interaction Patterns

Kirsten Westphal, Roland Petrasch

Department VI - Informatics and Media
Beuth Hochschule Berlin
University of Applied Sciences, Berlin, Germany
kirsten_westphal@yahoo.com, petrasch@beuth-hochschule.de

## Abstract

Patterns are accepted, proven and general solutions for recurring problems that can be applied in a specific and individual context. In order to leverage patterns the user, e.g. software developer, must understand the rules for the pattern application, i.e. for what kind of problems, under what circumstances and in what specific cases the pattern can be applied. A wrong pattern often lead to severe faults since they can affect not only the "microcosm" of a software, but also the large portions or complete aspects of a system's architecture, e.g. MVC.

This paper describes patterns for Human Computer Interaction (HCI patterns) and the creation of a rule-set in order to make the application of patterns easier in software projects. The (pattern application) rules aim to support the interdisciplinary communication, e. g. between graphic-designers, software engineers and usability experts. To reach that goal, general rules for the application of patterns are developed and modeled with UML activity diagrams. The rules focus on patterns for websites. Only a subset of available patterns are selected in order to provide a proof-of-concept. However, the approach can be used as a basis for further work and a road-map for individual and specific rule-sets that are useful also for other application domains and HCI platforms.

**Keywords:** Human computer interaction, HCI pattern, usability pattern, user interface, web-site usability, rule set, interactive system

## 1. Introduction

The analysis of HCI patterns and the development of a general rule-set that can be used as a starting point for concrete software projects for interactive systems consists of several steps: pattern selection, analysis and formalization, general rule creation, application and evaluation.

HCI patterns are published through Web repositories or collections ([8], [9], [10]), books ([1], [5]) and scientific papers ([7]). The focus regarding the research of HCI pattern collections is on the identification of recurrent solution of problems for designing websites, so that the pattern collections help to improve the ergonomic quality. Therefore, HCI patterns will be arranged, analyzed and evaluated. The results are used to create formal criteria and rules that describe the proper application of the HCI patterns. Criteria are specific for each pattern; they are the "atomic" modules for the rules and consists of conditions that must be met in order to apply that pattern. The rules then combines the criteria and presents them in a process-oriented format. In the end the rule-set is a formal operational guideline for the HCI patterns application[1]. Also anti-patterns [6] are used to evaluate and to improve the criteria and the rules.

In this paper five HCI patterns are selected in order to exemplify the approach. They are compared and analyzed. The rules describe the usage (or application) of the patterns during the user interface conception phase. The effect of this constructive quality measure are design decisions funded on well-known and accepted HCI patterns, thus avoiding arbitrariness and errors during the design process. A user interface design that is based on HCI patterns and documented accordingly is also easier to understand by many stakeholders of a projects, e.g. new development personnel, customer, usability engineer.

# 2. HCI Patterns

## 2.1 Pattern Selection

In general, patterns are considered as proven solutions for recurring problems. HCI patterns specify solutions for interactive systems. „Patterns communicate insights into design problems, capturing the essence of the problem and their solutions in a compact form. They describe the problem in depth, the rationale for the solution, [and] how to apply the solution" [1, p.19]. To ensure the generality or universality of the patterns, various aspects like guidelines, prin-

---

[1] The methodology to create the rule-set used the Hegelian dialectic [2] with the three dialectical stages: thesis, antithesis and synthesis [3]. The description of this methodology would go beyond the scope of this paper.

ciples (e.g. Shneiderman "eight golden rules" [4]), international norms (e.g. ISO 9241) and scientific facts like Fitts' law or G.A. Miller's concept of chunks[2] will be included.

For the analysis, five HCI patterns collections will be used: Jennifer Tidwell "Designing Interfaces" [5], Douglas K. van Duyne "The design of sites: patterns for creating winning web sites" [1], Anders Toxboe's UI patterns [9], Martijn van Welie's pattern library [10] and his scientific paper [7] and Yahoo! Design Patterns Library [8]. There were three criteria for selecting these collections: usage of categories, formal classification of the patterns and diversity. One collection will be introduced in a short form as an example.

## 2.2 Example: „Designing Interfaces"by Jennifer Tidwell

The collection of Jennifer Tidwell contains 94 patterns and nine subcategories: „What user do"; „Organizing the content: Information architecture and application structure";„Getting around: Navigation, signpost, way finding"; „Organizing the page: Layout of page elements"; „Doing things: Actions and commands"; „Showing complex data: trees, tables and other information graphics"; „Getting input from users: forms and controls"; „Builders and editors"; „Making it look good: Visual style and aesthetics". Except the category „what users do", all the patterns are organized in the following structure: „what" (what is the essence of the pattern); „use when" (further explanations); „why" (why to use the pattern); „how" (how to use the pattern and short description of use case); „examples" (examples for usage).

## 2.3 Anti-Patterns

HCI patterns try to extract patterns from successful systems in an abstract or general form. In contrast, HCI anti-patterns „must be identified in unsuccessful systems, and their absence shown in successful systems in order for them to qualify as anti-patterns" [6]. Anti-patterns can be specified in the following form (explained by the example "password-choice"):

1. "Symptoms and Consequences": Some user leaves a Web-Site, without completing the registration process, because of frustration by the password-choice.

---

[2] The Magical Number Seven, Plus or Minus Two according to Miller refers to the limited capacity of short-term memory of human beings: Only seven plus/minus two meaningful information units can be hold in the short term memory. However, later research results pointed out that the limitations of human memory cannot be defined by a simple constant and has a more dynamic character.

2. „Re-factored Solution": Use a help-button for more information.

3. „Benefits and Consequences": Well-informed users choose better passwords.

# 3. Developing the Rules

## 3.1 Pattern Comparison

In order to develop the rules, patterns of different collections are analyzed for similarities. Table 1 shows the comparison of some patterns that fulfill two criteria: the pattern exists in at least three collections. In this context the term "exists" means that there is a conformity in at least one special subcategory (use when - „Designing interfaces"; how – „welie.com" [7]; What's the Solution? - „yahoo-pattern-collection"[8]; Problem – „Design of Sites"; Solution – „ui-pattern.com" [9]). If there is a similarity the sign „✓" was chosen and if not „-".

| Pattern collection / Pattern name | "Designing Interfaces" | welie.com | yahoo-Pattern Sammlung | "Design of Sites" | ui-pattern.com |
|---|---|---|---|---|---|
| Auto-complete | Auto-completion | ✓ | ✓ | Predictive Input | ✓ |
| Breadcrumbs | ✓ | ✓ | ✓ | Location Breadcrumbs | ✓ |
| Card Stack | ✓ | Tabs | Navigation Tab | Tab Rows | Navigation Tab |
| Carrousel | Illustrated Choices | ✓ | ✓ | - | ✓ |
| Closable Panels | ✓ | Accordion | Accordion | - | Accordion Menu |
| Dropdown Chooser | ✓ | Fly-Out Menu | - | Drill-Down Options | Vertical Dropdown |
| Global Navigation | ✓ | Main Navigation | Top Navigation Bar | Navigation Bar | - |
| Grid-Based Layout | Visual Framework | ✓ | Page Grids | Grid Layout | - |
| Meaningful Error Messages | Same-Page Error Messages | Input Errors Message | - | ✓ | Input Feedback |
| Overview plus Detail | ✓ | Overview by Detail | - | Fast-Loading Images | Image Zoom |
| Account Registration | - | Registration | - | Sign in / New Account | ✓ |
| Alternative Views | ✓ | Printer-Friendly Page | - | Printable Pages | - |
| Calender Picker | - | Date Selector | ✓ | - | ✓ |
| Liquid Layout | ✓ | ✓ | - | Expanding Screen Width | - |

| Movable Panels | ✓ | - | Drag and Drop Modules | Direct Manipulation | - |
|---|---|---|---|---|---|
| Paging | - | ✓ | Search Pagination | - | Pagination |
| Preventing Errors | Input Hints/ Input Prompts | - | - | ✓ | Structured Format |
| Progress Bar | - | - | ✓ | ✓ | Completeness Meter |
| Prominent Done Button | ✓ | Action Button | - | Action Button | - |
| Right/ Left alignment | ✓ | Form | - | Clear Forms | - |
| Row Striping | ✓ | Alternating Row Colors | - | - | Alternating Row Colors |
| Wizard | ✓ | ✓ | - | - | ✓ |

Table 1: Comparison of HCI patterns collections

## 3.2 Example: Pattern Analysis and Formalization

In order to reduce ambiguities and to avoid semantic gaps patterns should be describe as precise, but also as concise as possible. Therefore a well-known (semi-)formal language is to be used as the pattern description language, e.g. the UML (Unified Modeling Language) and OCL (Object Constraint Language)[3]. The first step towards pattern formalization is the analysis of the patterns to gain a better understanding. In the second step the pattern is formalized. A verification is necessary as a third step in order to ensure the quality of the pattern and its description.

To demonstrate the analysis of the patterns, one particular pattern is analyzed as an example: *Account Registration* (Synonyms: *Registration, Sign in / New Account*). Welie differentiates between *Registration* ("Problem: The users repeatedly need to (re)enter a large amount of personal data" [10]) and *Login* ("Problem: The users need to identify themselves so that stored data about/of them can be used in the process they are in." [10]) For the sake of simplicity we assume that the *Registration* pattern covers these two functions: Registration and Login.

The application of this pattern helps to meet the criterion "suitability for the task" (ISO 9241 Part 110: Dialogue principles, [11]) because personal data of a logged-in user can be automatically used for default values, e.g. the e-mail address. Therefore the "ergonomic value" is self-evident. However, a user should not be forced to register himself if it is not necessary or desired: In many cases large parts of a web site can be used even if the user is not registered and logged-in.

---

[3] OCL is a side-effect-free, typed specification language. An OCL expression can be defined easily in the context of an UML model.

The analysis above showed that the patterns consists of several user interactions and should be formalized with a behavioral modeling language like UML activity diagram or state charts.

The following model shows a simplified *Registration* pattern as an UML activity diagram: The user can login with his or her user name and password. It is also possible to register (fill out the registration form). It is also possible to register without trying to login (not shown in the diagram). This process is a pattern, because it can be used in many different software systems, especially in web-applications. The UI designer needs decision support in order to apply HCI patterns according to the problem that has to be solved, i. e. a detailed description of the pattern should be provided. This decision support is shown below in the form of the rule set.

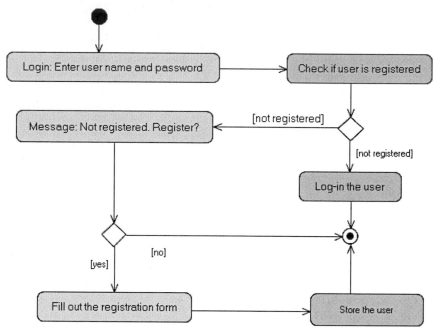

Figure 1: Activity diagram for the simplified *Registration* pattern (s. [12])

Using UML profiles, e. g. the MBUI and HCI Pattern profiles make the model-based approach even more powerful (s. [12]).

## 2.2 Example: Using an Anti-Pattern

The pattern *Overview plus Detail* is selected as an example for the use of an anti pattern. The patterns means that there is a detailed view next to the overview (often used for maps).

1. "Symptoms and Consequences": The need of a user depends on the context and situation. So, if only one view of an image is offered, it is possible that the needed information cannot be found. For this reason, the user can be frustrated by the application and try to find a better solution that meets hers/his expectations (e.g. another Web-Site).

2. Furthermore, a usual problem is a slow data transfer rate if one wants to load large images. So, another reason to choose other Web-Sites could be that it takes too long to load the files.

3. „Re-factored Solution": Reduce frustration by different views and include the problem of loading images in your preliminary considerations to design your Web-Site.

4. „Benefits and Consequences": The use of *Overview plus Detail* can increase the convenience of your Web-Site and the impact how users evaluate your Web-Site.

## 2.3 Example for the Pattern Consolidation

In order to reduce redundancy and to develop the rule set, the patterns had to be consolidated (analyze the pattern, eliminate redundant patterns or contradictions, synthesize similar patterns etc.). For demonstrating this procedure, we take a look at the pattern *Right/ Left Alignment*, which deals with the position of labeling text fields (e.g. putting the label left of the text field).

Rule #1: If input in a text field is part of the application, the distance of the label of the text field to the text field should not exceed 12 px.

Rule #2: If input in a text field is part of the application, the label of the text field and the text field do not necessarily have to be closely together, if this would violate the overall design or layout guidelines.

Rule #3 (consolidated): Distance of a label from text filed is exactly 12 px. Reason: Readability is more important than a good looking design.

## 2.4 The Rules

All results of the previous chapters were used to form the following rules.

1. Rule: User-oriented auto-complete of words

If all following criteria can be answered in the affirmative the use of *Auto-complete* is required. The criteria are as followed:

a) There is a possibility for entering.

b) *Auto-complete* is requested to extend a search word.

c) The input is – partly – foreseeable.

## 2. Rule: Show the structure of a Web-Site, which consists of hierarchical levels

If all following criteria can be answered in the affirmative the use of *Bread-crumbs[4]* is required. The criteria are as followed:

a) The Web-Site is hierarchically structured and has more than three levels deep.

b) There is no other kind of navigation, which allows a simpler navigation.

c) The Web-Site does not use Non-orientation as a stylistic device.

## 3. Rule: Use of tabs or closable Panels, if there are many items

If the criteria a) to c) can be answered in the affirmative the use of *Closable Panels[5]* or *Tabs* is required. Criteria d) is a special case (indicated by *), and should only be included, if d) is true. The criteria are as followed:

a) The visual clarity is complicated by many items.

b) The problem of visual clarity can be solved by grouping the elements.

c) The number of categories > 4.

d) If the user is using a Web-application to fulfill routine work, it is helpful to give the user a possibility for using the keyboard for control.

## 4. Rule: Consistency by the use of *Main Navigation* and *Grid-Based Layout*

If the following criteria can be answered in the affirmative the use of *Main navigation* and *Grid-Based Layout[6]* is required. The criteria are as followed:

a) Does the Web-Site consist of several pages (that also concludes Web-Sites consisting of one page, but needs to be scrolled by a vertical scroll bar to show the content below)?

b) Are there several navigation elements or items?

c) The avoidance of a main Navigation is not a consciously composed style device.

---

[4]*Breadcrumbs* (Synonym: *Location Breadcrumbs*) mean that the hierarchical path from home-/start-page to the current page is shown.
[5]*Closable Panels* (Synonyms: *Accordion, Accordion Menu*) deal with collapsible panels.
[6]*Grid-Based Layout* (Synonyms: *Visual Framework, Page Grid, Grid Layout*) signifies that a grid is used for aligning and positioning the graphic elements on the Web-Site.

d) The avoidance of grid-based layout is not a consciously composed style device.

## 5. Rule: Display complex image information by the use of different views and a printer-friendly version

Use the pattern *Alternative View*[7] if a) can be answered in the affirmative. If the criteria b) to d) can be answered in the affirmative, then the use of *Overview plus Detail* is required. The criteria are as followed:

a) Is the Web-Site printer-friendly?

b) Does the Web-Site consist of graphics/pictures/maps?

c) Is there a surplus profit for the user by the use of different views?

d) Are users with low download speed part of the target group for the Web-Site, too?

## 6. Rule: Organizing tasks and data

Use the pattern *Paging*[8] if a) can be answered in the affirmative. If the criterion b) can be answered in the affirmative the use of *Account Registration*[9] is required. If the criteria c) and d) can be answered in the affirmative use the pattern *Wizard*. If just the criterion e) is affirmed the use of the pattern *Progress Bar* is required. Use a combination of *Wizard* and *Progress Bar*, if c) to e) are affirmed. The criteria are as followed:

a) Does the displaying of the content within the screen consist of a long list of data, which does not fit on one page – without zooming?

b) Are the tasks long or complicated, and does the user repeatedly needs to (re)enter the same data?

c) Are the tasks long or complicated, and is the user also novice?

d) Is there an alternative possibility for experienced users to enter data?

e) Is the task long and consist of several sub-tasks respectively sections?

---

[7]*Alternative Views* (Synonyms: *Printer-friendly Page, Printable Pages*) deal with the offer of alternative views like a printer-friendly view. So, the user is able to print the content of a page without formatting problems.
[8]*Paging* (Synonyms: *Search Pagination, Pagination*) is often used in the context of searching in a long list of items. The list will be divided into several pages, and the user is able to select the pages by "next"- and "previous"- buttons.
[9]*Account Registration* (Synonyms: *Registration, Sign in/ New Account*) means that the user can be offered a possibility to store data, if the same data often has to be entered.

## 7. Rule: Include complexity of data, space to work and effectiveness by showing graphics at a time

If the criteria a) and b) can be answered in the affirmative the use of *Carrousel* is required. If the criteria a) to c) can be answered in the affirmative: use the pattern *Drop Down Chooser*. If just d) and e) is affirmed, the use of *Calendar Picker* is necessary. The criteria are as followed:

a) Is there a set of items to be selected?

b) Are the items graphics or pictures?

c) Is focusing on the essence important to the user?

d) Does the user want to select information based on a date?

e) Is there additionally also a possibility to enter data by a keyboard?

## 8. Rule: Preventing errors and support error recovery

If the criteria a) and b) can be answered in the affirmative the use of *Preventing Errors* is required. If just the criterion c) can be affirmed, use Meaningful *Error Messages*. The criteria are as followed:

a) Is it possible for the user to enter data?

b) Is there a certain kind of input expect from the user?

c) Is it possible that the user produces errors by entering the data?

## 9. Rule: Let the user customize the view

If the criterion a) can be answered in the affirmative the use of *Liquid Layout* is required. If the criteria b) and c) can be affirmed: use the pattern *Liquid Panels*. The criteria are as followed:

a) Is there any exclusion, for not resizing the page content, if the window was resized?

b) Does the Web-Site consist of separable panels, and a chronological order is not necessary?

c) Is it easy possible to restore the original state?

## 10. Rule: Enhance the communication with readability and visibility

If the criterion a) can be answered in the affirmative the use of *Row Striping* is required. If just the criterion b) can be affirmed: use the pattern *Right/ Left Alignment*, and if criterion c) can be answered in the affirmative: use *Prominent Done Button*. The criteria are as followed:

a) Is a table part of the Web-Site?

b) Is there a possibility for entering data in a text field?

c) Is there a task, which can be completed by a button?

## 2.5 Activity diagram

The rules will be formalized on the basis of the UML activity diagrams. Representative for the ten activity diagrams - that were built according to the number of rules - I select the diagram "Dealing with complex data". This diagram (shown in figure 2) is the most complex diagram of the ten and it is based on the pattern *Account Registration, Pagination, Progress Bar* and *Wizard*.

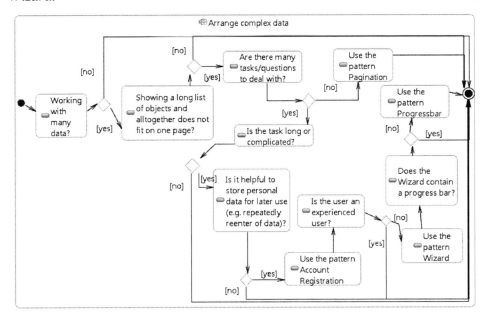

Figure 2: Activity diagram "Arrange complex data"

The first step to deal with is the Initial Node (black point at the left), which is the starting point for checking the usage of the pattern. Then different questions guide through the diagram. If the last node include "Use Pattern ... " the use of the pattern is required. Another possibility is a direct transition to the final node (black node with white border, at the right), without the node "Use Pattern ... ", then the usage of the pattern is not recommended. The diagram was built with the software Eclipse SDK Version: 3.5.1 and the Plug-In „UML2 Tools".

41

# 3. Conclusion

HCI patterns can be formalized in order to provide a more precise and concise definition. But also the application of HCI pattern must be formalized so that the UI designer has use HCI pattern effectively and efficiently. This is done by a rule set and process models for the HCI pattern application.

The generalities were derived gradually by analyzing and outlining five different pattern-collections. These results were used to extract criteria. By means of Anti-Patterns, the criteria were proven and afterwards increased by consolidation to develop generalities. As a result, ten generalities were developed, which are simple to use and understand for software developer and computer graphic artists, as well.

# References

[1] Duyne, Douglas K. van; Landay, James A.; Hong, Jason I.: The design of sites: patterns for creating winning web sites. 2. Auflage. Saddle River, NJ: Prentice Hall, 2007. ISBN 0-13-134555-9

[2] Hegel, Georg Wilhelm Friedrich: Wissenschaft der Logik. Schick, Friedrike u.a. [Hrsg.] Berlin: Akademie-Verlag 2002. ISBN-10: 3050037113

[3] Hügli, Anton; Poul Lübcke [Hrsg.]: Philosophie-Lexikon. Hamburg: Rowohlt 1997. ISBN 3-499-55453-4

[4] Shneiderman, Ben; Plaisant, Catherine: Designing the user interface. Strategies for effective human-computer interaction. 4. Auflage. Reading, MA [u.a.]: Addison Wesley Longman 2005. ISBN 0-321-19786-0

[5] Tidwell, Jenifer: Designing interfaces. Beijing [u.a.]: O'Reilly 2006. ISBN 978-0-596-00803-1

[6] Van Biljon, Judy; Kotzé, Paula; Renaud, Karen; McGee, Marilyn; Seffah, Ahmed: The use of anti-patterns in human computer interaction: wise or Ill-advised? Proceedings of the 2004 annual research conference of the South African institute of computer scientists and information technologists on IT research in developing countries, S.176-185. 4.-6. Oct, 2004

[7] Van Welie, Martijn: Task-Based User Interface Design. Academisch Proefschrift. Amsterdam: Vrije Universiteit 2001.

[8] Yahoo Design Pattern Library: http://developer.yahoo.com/ypatterns/, Accessed on 22.01.2011

[9]  UI Patterns: http://ui-patterns.com/patterns, Accessed on 22.01.2011

[10] Martijn van Welie: http://welie.com/, Accessed on 22.01.2011

[11] ISO 9241-110. Ergonomics of human-system interaction -- Part 110: Dialogue principles. ISO, 2006

[12] Petrasch, R.: Model Based User Interface Development and HCI Patterns: An Example with the Registration-Pattern. In: Songsak Rongviriyapanich, Roland Petrasch (Eds.): Proceedings of Software Engineering and Quality Assurance. Technical Report #1, Thammasat University, Bangkok, Thailand & Beuth Hochschule für Technik, Berlin, Germany, 2012

# Model Based User Interface Development and HCI Patterns: An Example with the View-/Edit-Pattern

Roland Petrasch

Beuth Hochschule für Technik Berlin
Fachbereich VI Informatik und Medien
Luxemburger Str. 10
13353 Berlin, Germany

petrasch@beuth-hochschule.de

**Abstract**

This paper presents the View-Edit-Pattern (VE-Pattern) as an example for HCI patterns in conjunction with model-based or model-driven software development for interactive systems, known as model based user interface design (MBUID). It also shows parts of a MBUID and HCI patterns profile based on the UML Superstructure. The profiles extend the UML (class model, state chart etc.) and can be used as a lightweight metamodel: The Stereotypes are used in application models in order to take user interface aspects into account. The VE-Pattern demonstrates the advantages of the approach. However, MBUID also raise some critical questions, e.g. the expressiveness of the modeling language.

**Keywords**

Model driven development, model-based user interface design, MBUI, MBUID, MDA, HCI patterns, usability, ergonomics, Registration Pattern

## 1. Model Based User Interface Design

OMG'S MDA (Model Driven Architecture) uses the concepts *platform*, *metamodel* and *transformation*. On one hand, a platform independent model (PIM) in the context of MBUID is a user interface model that abstracts from a concrete (G)UI framework or technology (e. g. HTML5, Android, Swing). On the other hand, a platform specific model (PSM) contains aspects of a concrete UI framework or technology, e. g. canvas elements for a HTML page, layout data for a mobile Android app or an ActionListener for a Swing client. While PIM and PSM base on metamodels, a platform specific implementation (PSI) only needs the (technological) platform specification, e.g. HTML documents, XML layout documents or Java code for Swing clients.

The platform concept of OMG's MDA is relative: After the transformation of a PIM to a PSM, the PSM becomes a PIM for the next transformation(s) (PIM PSM transformation) until a PSI is generated (PIM PSI transformation). This implies a forward engineering approach.

In this context a light-weight approach based on the profile mechanism of the UML Superstructure is is used, i.e. no new metamodel or new metamodel elements are necessary since a profile extends existing UML elements with Stereotypes. Two profiles have been developed: A MBUI profile that provides general elements for user interfaces and interactive systems and a HCI pattern profile that makes is possible to define reusable HCI patterns.

For more than 20 years several languages have been available for this purpose, e,g, *User Action Notation* [5]. More recent approaches employ UML profiles or languages based on meta models that conform to MOF with some similarities to the UML. Examples of light-weight approaches [Is this a proper expression?] with UML profiles are GUILayout [1] and Wisdom [9].

In the past, several light-weight and heavy-weight approaches have been developed. A more heavy-weight approach is UMLi [11] with its own meta model (as an UML extension).

It is in the nature of things that the usage of MBUID approaches are intrinsically tied to regulations (and lead to restrictions) when it comes to modeling and transformation: Specific model languages have to be employed; moreover, the abstract and concrete syntax as well as the its semantics are also specific for a type of applications or technologies.

For instance UWE [7] employs navigation models that are represented by a UML class diagram and specific stereotypes for Web applications, e.g. <>. The advantage is the clear and unambiguous modeling scheme that comes with approaches like UWE. However, flexibility is limited since no other diagram types (or languages) can be employed other than those prescribed, without risking to put the benefits at stake. What happens if the modeling language (based on an UML profile or a metamodel) is not sufficient for the application development? Many more questions arise concerning aspects like the following (just to mention a few):

- Abstractness: The UI models (or description languages) can be/operate on a very abstract level (like in the case of Xforms [13], in which a trigger can be a button, a hypertext link or a spoken command) or very concrete, e.g. the stereotype <<button>> in UWE.

- Conformity to standards: Heavy-weight approaches that define their own meta model and employ a specific transformation language for

MBUID do not follow accepted standards, like OMG's MOF, QVT or UML. The consequences must be taken into account.

- Transformation language characteristics: The quality of these languages differ concerning orthogonality, regularity, simplicity, extensibility (just to mention some).

A look at HCI patterns in conjunction with MBUID shows another interesting however challenging aspect of model based approaches for interactive systems.

# 2. HCI patterns meet Model Driven Development

HCI patterns have a history of more than ten years [2], [12], but mostly they have been described at an informal (or semi-formal) level. The variety of HCI or usability patterns is immense: There are application-specific HCI patterns, like game patterns [4], and general purpose patterns for high level specification or detailed design [8]. Many HCI pattern libraries that can be found on [6] [Incomplete sentence]. Description languages for patterns range from textual notation to XML-based formal languages, e.g. the *Pattern Language Markup Language* (PLML) [3].

Even in the context of UML the decision for the "right" diagram type can be a challenge. To exemplify this, let us take a look at a simple profile for MBUID (see *Fig. 1*). It shows typical stereotypes of interactive systems modeling, e.g. <<Dialog>>. Note that some stereotypes extend more than one UML meta class, e.g. <<Dialog>> can be employed in state machines and in class diagrams.

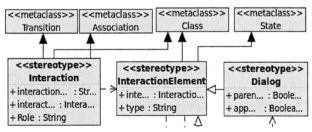

Fig. 1: Detail of an UML profile for MBUID

Another profile is provided for HCI patterns: It provides the modeler the ability to define a pattern in the context of an UML package (see Fig. 2). Elements of a pattern can also be marked as a(n) (input) parameter, i. e. it must be provided by the user of the pattern.

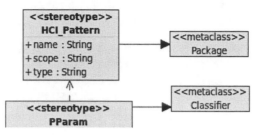

Fig. 2: Detail of an UML profile for HCI patterns

Now we can define HCI patterns in the context of the MBUI profile. *Fig. 3* shows the YNC pattern ("Yes/No/Cancel" [10], [14]) as a class diagram: From a source dialog an exit interaction leads to feedback dialog. From there three interactions are possible for the user: Yes, No or Cancel.

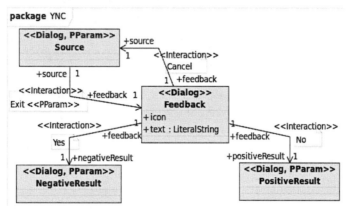

Fig. 3: The YNC pattern defined with the MBUI profile and the HCI pattern profile (s. [14])

Class diagrams are quite common for MBUID. However, there are limitations, e. g. the focus is on structural aspects and not on the dynamic or behavioral viewpoint. The following model illustrates another HCI pattern as a state machine ("View / Read-only and Edit") in which the same profiles are applied (see *Fig. 4*).

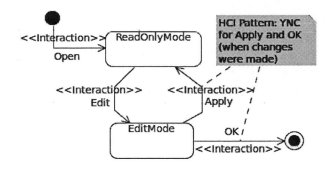

Fig. 4: The VE-Pattern („View / Edit") as a state machine

This pattern provides two different states for one dialog that is initially in a read-only state. User interaction (e. g. with a click on an edit-button) changes the state and data can be altered.

Although a state machine is appropriate for the modeling of this particular pattern, the well-known disadvantages must be considered, e. g. problems with inheritance. In other words, every UML diagram type (and probably every modeling language in general) has its advantages and disadvantages for MBUID and HCI patterns.

# 4. Summary

Up till the present, we see just the beginning of MBUID in conjunction with HCI patterns in practice. More research and practical experiences are necessary in order to provide evaluation results and to create appropriate specification and development languages. A key success factor for both, MBUI and HCI patterns lies in the symbiosis effect: Reusable HCI patterns that are used in a model-driven development approach will lead to better usability for interactive systems, especially when it comes to aspects like consistency or standardization; the productivity of software development project can also be increased.

A powerful tool chain, open and extensible MBUI and HCI pattern languages and environments and qualified personnel are necessary in order to make usage of MBUID and HCI patterns in real-world projects. Standardization is another key success factor, e.g. with the help of OMG's Model Driven Architecture (MDA).

# References

1. Blankenhorn, K.: A UML Profile for GUI Layout. FH Furtwangen, Diplomarbeit, 2004

2. Coram, T. and Lee, J.: Experiences -- A Pattern Language for User Interface Design. In: Pattern Languages of Program Design, Proceedings, 1996

3. Fincher, S.: Perspective on HCI Patterns: Concepts and tools (introducing PLML). In: Interfaces (56), British HCI Group, CHI 2003 Workshop Rep., 2003, pp. 27-28

4. Folmer, E.: Usability Patterns in Games. Futureplay 2006 Conference, London, Ontario, Canada, 3. Oct. 2006

5. Hartson, H. R., Siochi, A. C. and Hix, D.: The UAN: A User-Oriented Representation for Direct Manipulation Interface Designs, ACM Transactions on Information Systems, Vol. 8, No. 3, July 1990, pp. 181-203

6. HCI Patterns website: http://www.hcipatterns.org

7. Koch, N.: Software Engineering for Adaptive Hypermedia Systems. Diss., LMU Munich, 2001

8. Mahemoff, M. J. and Johnston, L. J.: Usability Pattern Languages: the "Language" Aspect. In: M. Hirose:, Human-Computer Interaction: Interact '01, Tokyo, pp. 350-358

9. Nunes, N. J.: Object Modeling for User-Centered Development and User Interface Design: The Wisdom Approach, Universidade da Madeira, Diss., 2001

10. Petrasch, R.: Model Based User Interface Design: Model Driven Architecture und HCI Patterns. In: GI Softwaretechnik-Trends, Band 27, Heft 3, 2007, pp. 5-10

11. Pinheiro da Silva, P. and Paton, N. W.: *User Interface Modeling in UMLi.* IEEE Software, July/Aug. 2003, pp. 62-69

12. Tidwell, J.: Interaction Patterns. In: Pattern Languages of Program Design, Proceedings, Monticello, 1998

13. W3C: XForms. W3C-standard, Vers 1.1, 2009

14. Roland Petrasch: Model Based User Interface Design: Model Driven Architectureund HCI Patterns. In: GI Softwaretechnik-Trends, Mitteilungen der Gesellschaft für Informatik, Band 27, Heft 3, Sept. 2007, S. 12-17

# Productivity and Maintainability in Extreme Programming and Waterfallbased Projects

Charinya Klakhang[1] , Songsak Rongviriyapanish[2],
Taweesup Apiwattanapong[3]

Computer Science Dep., Thammasat University [1,2] Pathumthani, Thailand

National Electronic and Computer Technology Center[3], Pathumthani, Thailand

charinya.klakhang@nectec.or.th[1], rongviri@cs.tu.ac.th[2]

taweesup.apiwattanapong@nectec.or.th[3]

## Abstract

Agile software development is gaining popularity, as it responds wel[1]l to frequent changes in user requirements. However, the question of whether the lack of comprehensive documentation emphasis in Agile methodologies affects the maintainability of software and the productivity of developers in the long run is still controversial. In this paper we examine the productivity and the maintainability of software developed using an Agile methodology in comparison with those using a nonagile methodology. The study in this research uses two productivity measurement and three maintainability measures. The results show that the productivity during development using an Agile methodology is 50% higher than that using a nonagile methodology, whereas the maintainability is comparable for both software developed by an Agile methodology and a nonagile methodology.

## Keywords

Agile Methodology, Waterfall, Extreme Programming (XP), Productivity, and Maintainability

# 1. Introduction

Nowadays, many software development project focus on customer satisfaction, quick adaptation to changes, and flexibility. Therefore, Agile software development has become popular because it responds well to frequent changes in user requirements and focuses on the interaction among stakehold-

51

ers collaborating to achieve high productivity and deliver high-quality software. Extreme Programming (XP), a well-known Agile development model [1,2], has many practices that improve the quality of work such as pair programming, planning game and test driven development. Moreover, Agile methodologies give more emphasis on working software than comprehensive documentation thus having the advantage of saving development time to create and update many documents, so developers can release products faster.

Nevertheless, XP, with Agile development in general, is criticized as having only simple software design and insufficient documentation, the question of whether the lack of this emphasis affects the maintainability of software developed using Agile methodologies and the productivity of the developers in the long run is still controversial. There are not enough empirical evidences to support either side of this argument. This research, thus, examines the productivity and the maintainability of software developed using an Agile methodology, Extreme Programming (XP), in comparison with those using a Non-Agile methodology, Waterfall-based model, a model that loosely follows the Waterfall model.

The study uses both quantitative and qualitative metrics. The qualitative metrics were collected from surveys and interviews of development teams and the quantitative metrics consist of two productivity measures and three maintainability measures.

In this study, we compared productivity and maintainability between the Extreme Programming model (Agile) and Waterfall-based model (Non-Agile) applied to two small and medium size software development project. In addition, we used the Extreme Programming Evaluation Framework (XP-EF) [3] to evaluate the characteristics of the project teams in order to select only teams with the similar characteristics for the comparison study.

# 2. Background

This section presents background material on Extreme Programming, the Waterfall model, software metrics and the XP-EF framework.

## 2.1 Agile Methodology

Agile methodologies [1-5] are sets of software development processes that are classified as iterative and incremental models. They emphasize customer satisfaction and respond to changes in requirements. The Manifesto for Agile software development, which portrays the important principles of Agile method includes [6]:

• Individual and interactions over processes and tools.

• Working software over comprehensive documentation.

• Customer collaboration over contract negotiation.

• Responding to change over following a plan.

There are many Agile methods based on the Agile Manifesto such as Extreme Programming (XP) [2], Scrum [7], Crystal methods [8], Feature Driven Development (FDD) [9]. In this project, we selected the XP model as an Agile method to study because it has clear development practices and, is a well-known Agile method. [2, 10]

## 2.2 Extreme Programming (XP)

Extreme programming (XP) was developed by Kent Beck. XP has already been proven at many companies to be successful because it stresses on customer satisfaction. The methodology is designed to deliver the software your customer needs when it is needed. [25]. The 12 practices of XP are explained below. [2,11, 12]

• Pair programming: a programming technique that two programmers work together at one computer on the same task[13]. The purpose of pair programming is to increase team productivity, improve the quality of source code and raise job satisfaction and confidence.

• Common code ownership: all team members may change anywhere in the code, e.g., no one owns any piece of code individually. Anyone can edit without asking the original writer because their code follows the same coding standard. The purpose of common code ownership is that a team member can update the whole project.

• Planning game: at the beginning of a project, a release and an iteration, team members write user stories that summarize and describe requirements from customers. Then, customers choose the most valuable user stories (probably more than one) to implement in a short iteration. The purpose of planning game is for team members to move requirements in and out of the plan together based on customer needs.

• Frequent small releases: the software is produced and delivered in small releases to customers. Customers can provide feedback after they try it out. The team should not attempt to add precipitate requirement.

• Continuous integration: XP divides an implementation to several iteration. As a result, There are many small pieces of the software to be synchronized and tested. Team members should keep code in a repository for easy update.

• Refactoring code: software should be rewritten and redesigned when code smell, i.e., any symptom in the source code that possibly indicates a deeper

53

problem is detected [14]. Refactoring is the technique for restructuring source code to make it easy to understand, such as removing duplicate code, large method, large class, lazy class, feature envy, renaming classes or methods and clarifying software architecture. The objective is to increase readability and maintainability.

- On-site customer: XP project requires communication with the customers. The customers should be available for development, such as to answer question and give more explanation of unclear requirements.

- Coding standard: the team members must agree on standards of coding to be used. Using standards lead to easy implementation, refactoring and understanding of code.

- Sustainable pace: the team members should be happy working. In the planning game, they estimate acceptable time to develop. They should work for 40 hours per week.[4]

- Test-driven development: a software development technique that uses short development iterations based on pre-written test cases that define desired improvements or new functions [14].

- Simple design: the software development concept that responds to change because the development prepares to increase function needed by customers. Developers will rewrite and redesign code using refactoring practice. At the beginning of an iteration, the design and implementation should be flexible and of low complexity.

- System metaphor: Common language that is used to explain the project by doing metaphor with the previous project.

The development team should accept and be willing to follow XP practices. However, in this experiment, some practices were practiced less than 100%, which will be explain in more detail in the next section.

## 2.3 Waterfall Model

The Waterfall model is originally invented by Winston W. Royce in 1970. This model assumes that requirements remain static throughout a project and emphasizes having documents to support each development step. Waterfall development has distinct goals for each phase. The process has 5 steps: requirement, design, implementation, integration and operation and maintenance.

Software industry in Thailand generally develops software with emphasis on documentation based on Waterfall model such as user requirement specification, testing document and design diagram. The developers spend time to create and update them. In addition, changing requirement is hardly negotiated. However, the advantage of more documents is increasingly reliance of maintainers who never develop existing project before. As a result, we select the Waterfall-based model to compare with Extreme Programming model.

## 2.4 Quantitative Metrics

Quantitative metrics are available for almost every aspect of software development. In this context we focus on two types of metrics:

- Productivity metrics: The generally accepted measures for the productivity of a software engineer involve two measures: size per effort. Size can calculate by line of code (LOC) and function point (FP) [15].

- Maintainability metrics: Many software projects use maintainability measurement such as coding effort, design effort, percentage of modules changes, classes changes, classes added [12]. In addition, Fenton presents the maintainability metrics in external view such as mean or median time to repair, ratio of total change implement time to total number of changes implemented, number of unsolved problems, time spent on unsolved problems, percentage of changes that introduce new faults and number of modules modified to implement a change [16].

## 3. Research Method

The goal of this research is to compare the productivity and maintainability between Extreme Programming and Waterfall-based models when applied to small and medium- size software development. To achieve the goal, this research conducts an experiment involving two software development projects that have the same requirements and customers with different software process models. The first project follows the Extreme Programming model. The other follows the Waterfall-based model. Each project is divided into 2 phases: development and maintenance phases. Figure 1 shows the flow of each project in this experiment.

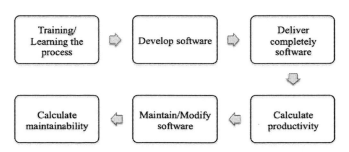

Figure 1. Steps of Experiment

## 3.1 Empirical project development based on XP

This project started with developers training in Extreme Programming techniques. These developers were then tested for their understanding of XP practices by using questionnaires. Those who passed the test were assumed to be ready to implement project using XP. The developers then started developing a project by following the XP practices. They produced these artifacts:

• user stories

• test cases

• data dictionary

• coding standard and technical document

• user manual, source code

All artifacts were checked before submitting to the repository for the maintenance phase. Before the software was accepted by customers, we ran test cases on the software when the software passed all test cases the project is completed. Next, we calculated and analyzed the productivity measurement. Then we checked whether the developers conform to XP practices. The whole XP Processes are shown in Figure 2.

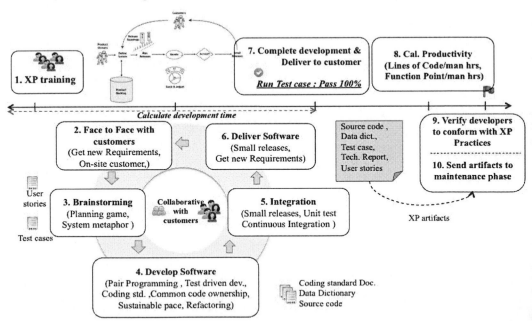

Figure 2.   Empirical project on XP

In each iteration of XP development, the developers wrote user story cards that are sticked on the board. This user story board is divided into three columns. The first column, "Non checkout", groups user stories waiting for development in next iterations. The second column, "check out", contains user stories under implementation in this iteration that are not completed. When the implementation is finished, its user story is moved to the third column, "Done".

## 3.2 Empirical project development based on Waterfall

Developers divide their work based on their roles. First, the developers summarized all requirements from customers and produced a user requirement specification. After that, they designed the system architecture, components and database models. For instance, They wrote use case diagrams to explain the requirements. In addition, they also created E-R diagrams, Sequence diagrams and Activity diagrams of the entire project in this stage. They implemented the software by following the documents and used unit tests regularly. When completing all the components, the developers integrated all the pieces together and began an integration test.

Finally, the developer delivered the customers the complete software when all of these stages finished. Figure 3 shows the flow of this project.

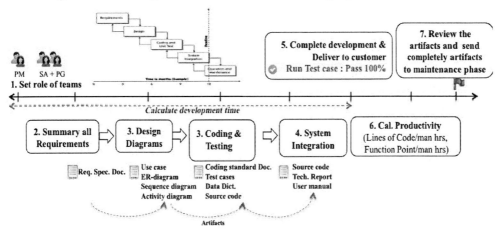

Figure 3.   Empirical project on Waterfall-based

The artifacts that were checked and submitted to the repository include:

• user requirement specification

• use case diagram, activity diagram, E-R diagram

• testing document

• data dictionary

• coding standard and technical document

• user manual,source code

The project that uses Waterfall-based model produces more artifacts than that of XP model does. However, the development time of the Waterfall-based project is greater than that of XP. At the end of this step, we calculated and analyzed the productivity of this project. Maintainability metrics will be calculated in the next step.

## 3.3 Empirical project maintenance

In the maintenance phase, groups of maintainers obtained the artifacts produced by each development project. The documentation produced by the XP process was less than that of the Waterfall-based process. The two groups were given similar requirements for changes and new functionality. They then studied and modified the existing artifacts. Figure 4 shows the process flow in the maintenance phase.

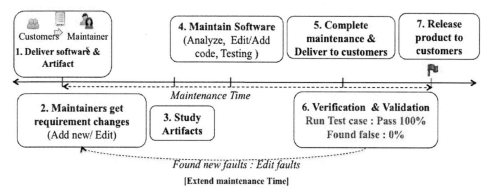

Figure 4. Empirical project maintenance

Finally, after all the changes were completed, the maintainability metrics were calculated.

# 4. Experiment

The goal of this experiment is to compare the productivity of the development teams and the maintainability of the software products between two projects that use two different development models. Thus, this experiment has an independent variable, the development model, that has two values: XP and Waterfall-based models. The dependent variables are the productivity of the development teams and the maintainability of the software products. Other factors are controlled to be similar for both projects as much as possible.

58

The first subsection shows the characteristic of both projects and the similarities between them. The second one shows the productivity and maintainability metrics used in this experiment.

## 4.1 Project Characteristics

In this experiment, the Extreme Programming Evaluation Framework (XP-EF) [3,18] was used to demonstrate the characteristics of both projects. XP-EF is a standard framework for understanding the similaries and differences among several different environments.

Specifically, this experiment uses the sociological and developmental factors, which are a part of XP-EF context factors, to describe the two projects.

Tables I show the project descriptions and their sociological factors. According to the data in these tables, both projects are very similar sociologically.

| Project name | Project management software 1 | Project management software 2 |
|---|---|---|
| Software Process | XP model | Waterfall-based model |
| Description | Project management software used internally by Software Engineering laboratory that has 20-30 users. The project started after developers studied XP practice. The development was divided into 6 iterations. The end of development, the project must have output as expected results in test cases. | Project management software used internally by Software Engineering laboratory that has 20-30 users. The requirement are similar to project 1, and the customers use the same, After the development is successful, we have much documentation to support the project |
| Software Classification | Web application | Web application |
| Sociological Factor | | |
| Team size | 4 + 1 SA | 4 + 1 SA |
| Team Education level | Bachelor's degree: 4 Master's degree: 1 | Bachelor's degree: 3 Master's degree: 2 |
| Experiment level of Team | < 10 year: 1 < 5 year: 4 | < 10 year: 1 < 5 year: 4 |
| Domain Expertise | Medium | Medium |
| Language Expertise | High (OO) | High (OO) |

Table I: Project descriptions and their sociological factors

The Polar chart, shown in Figure 5, shows the development factors of the two projects. The solid line represents the developer characteristics of the XP project; whereas the dotted line represents the developer characteristics of the Waterfall-based project. The data from this chart shows that both projects are similar with respect to these development factors. In addition, the polar chart can also indicate the extent to which a project is suited for Agile practices. The closer to the center the point on each axis is, the more suitable for Agile practices the project becomes [11]. Therefore, the data from this chart also shows that these projects are suitable for Agile practices.

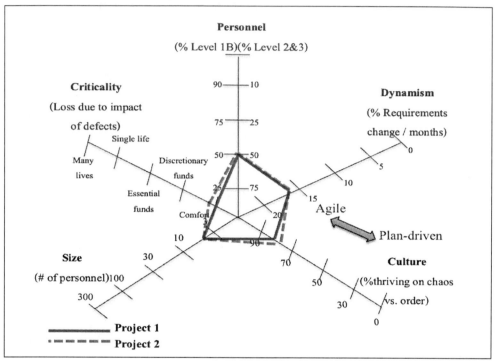

Figure 5 Development Factor of Project 1 [19,20]

XP-EF personnel factor uses Cockburn personnel levels [17] to classify the expertise of developers. Table II shows these personnel levels.

| Level | Team member characteristics |
|---|---|
| 3 | Able to revise a method, breaking its rules to fit an unprecedented new situation. |
| 2 | Able to tailor a method to fit a precedent new situation. |
| 1A | With training, able to perform discretionary method steps such as sizing stories to fit increments, composing pattern, compound refactoring, or complex COTS integration. With experience, can become Level 2. |
| 1B | With training, able to perform procedural method steps such as coding a simple method, simple refactoring, and following coding standards and configuration management procedures, or running test. With experience, can master some Level 1A skills. |

60

| -1 | May have technical skills but unable or unwilling to collaborative or follow shared method. |
|---|---|

Table II: Personnel levels proposed [17]

In the maintenance phase, the maintainers were assigned to modify – editing old requirements and adding new requirements – the both piece of software. The maintainers can use all the artifacts to study for maintenance.

## 4.2 Productivity Metrics

There are two productivity metrics that we selected to measure. The code artifact was taken from the source code the repository. This quantitative metrics are described below.

- Total Line of Code (TTR) per Effort: Count the total source lines of code except blank lines and comment lines per the total count of the man-month that software development takes from setup until delivery. A higher value is preferred. [11]

    P1 = TTR / Effort

- Total Unadjusted Function Point (UFP) per Effort: It measure a software project by quantifying the information processing functionality associated with major external data or control input, output, or file types [21]. Count the Unadjusted Function Point (UFP) per the total count of the man-month. A higher value is preferred.

    P2 = UFP / Effort

## 4.3 Maintainability Metrics

The metrics are the kind of quantitative metrics. We present two maintainability measurements.

- Total of Time to Repair (TR) per Class Changes: Average amount of time to study artifacts ,modify and test the software product per Class Changes of the modification. A lower value is preferred [22].

    MT1 = TR / Classes Changes

- Ratio of New Faults Made at Revision (RNF) per Unit Volume: Count the number of new faults per class changes. This metric presents stability of software that bears on the risk of an unexpected effect of modification. [23] A lower value is preferred.

    MT2 = RNF / Classes Changes

61

# 5. Results And Discussion

In this section, we analyze two kinds of metrics. Firstly the qualitative metrics such as survey, interview and observation. Secondly, quantitative metrics that are productivity and maintainability measurement.

## 5.1 Qualitative Metrics

We observe that the customers were satisfied with the XP resulting project and team's work. Moreover, the XP developers were satisfied that the process emphasizes the software more than the documentation. However, we also notice that it is easier to train Agile practices to inexperience developers but some experience developers tend to resist some XP practices, e.g. pair programming, Collective Code Ownership and Test-first development because they have to change their style. In this experiment, the percentage of using XP practices varies. All practices were used greater than 60% of development process. Refactoring code was used the lowest because the limitation of developer skill. When developers use more refactoring code, the code will be more readable and maintainable.

All XP artifacts were used, whereas some Waterfall-based artifacts were used. Moreover, the Waterfall-based developers were unsatisfied with frequently updated the documentation.

## 5.2 Quantitative Metrics

Productivity: The results shown in Table III showed that both productivity metrics of the XP project was higher than the Waterfall-base project. The productivity calculation used lines of code and function point.

The key to enhanced productivity in the XP project is refactoring, small release, pair programming (code reviews) and continuous integration. First of all, code refactoring was improved for readability, efficiency or maintainability. However, after refactoring is done, the code must pass entire test suites. Continuous integration discovers the defects early, thus, reduces the effort of fixing them. However, the developers wrote a set of tests and used an integration test also. In addition, pair programming and code reviews in this project served to reduce the risk of losing a developer, others could be instead the task.

On the other hand, in the Waterfall-based team, customers were involved at the inception of the project determined requirements and a contractual agreement. Developers wrote all documents before coding. Then customers changed some requirements, maybe after they acquired the finally product, developers need to redesign significantly and edit their documents.

Maintainability: By analyzing the results in Table III, the maintainability metrics that were measured by total time to repair and number of new faults made at revision. Both of XP are higher than Waterfall-based project. That mean, the measurement of the Waterfall-based is better than that the XP although the differences of both were little. Thus, The maintainability is comparable for both pieces of software developed by XP and Waterfall-based methods.

In this experiment, both developers constructed to different artifacts. However, the artifacts conformed with the standard template or definition that was approved by the project manager.

Documentation is the basic artifact that the maintainers may use. Although the number of artifacts of Waterfall-based project are greater than documentation from the XP project, in our survey, entire documentation of the Waterfall-based project was unnecessary to maintainers. While documentation of XP is sparse – often limited to source code and a set of user stories [2], but in this project we added some necessary artifacts such as set of test cases, data dictionary, and technical document to support in the maintenance phase.

| Model | P1 | P2 | MT 1 | MT 2 |
|---|---|---|---|---|
| | Productivity | | Maintainability | |
| X1 (XP) | 0.10 | 16.84 | 0.75 0 | 0.25 |
| X2 (Waterfall-based) | 0.06 | 9.23 | 0.737 | 0.237 |
| Model Overcome | X1 | X1 | X2 | X2 |

Table III: Results as values of metrics

# 6. Conclusion and Future Plans

We evaluated comparative analysis of productivity and maintainability between the XP process and Waterfall-based process. The productivity during development using XP is higher than that using Waterfall-based model, whereas the maintainability is comparable for both pieces of software developed by XP and Waterfall-based model. However, XP are unsuitable for all projects. Developers must consider the characteristics of the project to ensure that XP is appropriate. Moreover, the artifacts are important for maintenance. Therefore, developers should be aware of the artifacts.

In the future work, we plan to gather more data from the XP project and the Waterfall-based project to statistically approve the comparative maintainability between Agile and Non-Agile model in a larger project.

# References

1.  Craig Larman, Agile & Iterative Development - A Manager's guide, Addison-Wesley, 2004.
2.  K Beck. Extreme programming explained - embrace change, Addison - Wesley 2000.
3.  L. Williams, W. Krebs, L. Layman, A. Anto´n, P. Abrahamsson, "Toward a Framework for Evaluating Extreme Programming", presented at Empirical Assessment in Software Eng. (EASE) 2004, Edinburgh, 2004.
4.  Mira Kajko-Mattsson, Grace A. Lewis, Dave Siracusa, Taylor Nelson, Nedapin, Michael Heydt, Jason Nocks, Harry Snee, Long-term Life Cycle Impact of Agile Methodologies, ICSM, IEEE Society: 2006, 422-425.
5.  Naresh Jain, Offshore Agile Maintenance in AGILE 2006 Conference, IEEE Computer Society 2006.
6.  The Manifesto for Agile Software Development: http://agilemanifesto.org/.
7.  Ken Schwaber andMike Beedle. Agile Software Development with Scrum. Alan R. Apt, 2001.
8.  Alistair Cockburn. "CrystalClear: A Human - Powered Methodology for Small Teams". Addison - Wesley Professional, 2004.
9.  Stephen R Palmer and John M. Felsing. A Practical Guide to Feature Driven Development. Prentice Hall, 2002.
10. Kent Beck and Cynthia Andres. Extreme Programming Explained: Embrace Change. Addison-Wesley, 2nd edition, 2004.
11. Sato, D., Bassi, D., Bravo, M., Goldman, A., and Kon, F. (2006). Experiences tracking agile projects: an empirical study. Journal of the Brazilian Computer Society, Special Issue on Experimental Software Engineering, 12(3): 45–64.
12. Harald Svensson, Martin Host. "Introducing an Agile Process in Software Maintenance and Evolution Organization", Proceeding of the 9th European Conference on Software Maintenance and Reengineering, CSMR 2005, IEEE Society: 2005.

13. Linda B. Sherrell, Jeff J. Robertson. Pair programming and agile software development: experiences in a college setting, Journal of Computing Sciences in Colleges, Volume 22, Issue 2, December 2006.

14. Wikipedia., "Refactoring", http://en.wikipedia.org/wiki.

15. Sharpe, J.L. Cangussu, J.W., A productivity metric based on statistical pattern recognition, Computer Software and Applications Conference, 29th Annual International, 26-28 July 2005.

16. Norman E. Fenton, Software Metrics: A Rigorous Approach, Chapman & Hall, Ltd., London, UK, 1991.

17. A. Cockburn, Agile Software Development. Reading, Massachusetts: Addison Wesley Longman, 2001.

18. L. Williams, W. Krebs, and L.Layman, "Extreme Programming Evaluation Framework for Object Oriented Languages -- Version 1.3," North Carolina State University, Raleigh, NC Computer Science TR-2004-11, April7. 2004.

19. B. Boehm, "Software Risk Management: Principles and Practices," IEEE Software, no.pp. 32-41, January 1991.

20. B. Boehm and R. Turner, "Using Risk to Balance Agile and Plan-Driven Methods," IEEE Computer, vol. 36, no.6, pp..57-66, June 2003.

21. Barry Boehm, "COCOMO II Model Definition Manual", University of Southern California.

22. Quint2 (Quality in Information Technology) is a Dutch framework for software quality, extending ISO 9126, available at: http://www.serc.nl/quint-book

23. ISO/IEC 9126-3: "Software engineering -- Product quality -- Part 3: Internal metrics", 2003.

24. Krishan K. Aggarwal, Yogesh Singh, Jitender Kumar Chhabra., "An Integrated Measure of Software Maintainability", Reliability and Maintainability Symposium, 2002. Proceedings. Annual, 2002.

25. Extreme programming, http://www.extremeprogramming.org.

# Model-Driven Software Development with Xtext

Max Goltzsche

Beuth Hochschule Berlin,
University of Applied Sciences

## Abstract

The Model-Driven Software Development (MDSD) promises the development of high-quality software products with uniform changeable architectures. Its feasibility and work flow are evaluated on the basis of the award winning Eclipse utility Xtext by developing three Domain-Specific Languages (DSL) and generators to model and generate runnable Create-Read-Update-Delete (CRUD) web applications of the Java Enterprise Edition platform.

# 1. Introduction

The development of multi-tier applications requires the implementation of code in different tiers. The architecture's concept has to be realized in the same way in every use case that has to be implemented. Often this doesn't happen because the roles of programmer and architect are held by many different people not sharing the same knowledge or the application grows over the time inconsistently, it becomes a brownfield. Additionally, often the code contains repetitions which cannot be removed due to the borders of the used language.

## 1.1 Goal

In contrast the Model-Driven Software Development (MDSD) offers the possibility to develop software systems with homogeneous architectures that can be changed consistently (from [1], pp. 13). Thus feasibility and work flow of the MDSD concept are evaluated on the basis of the award winning Eclipse utility Xtext.

## 1.2 Structure of the Report

After the introduction the first part gives a short overview of the MDSD concepts and Model-Driven Architecture (MDA). The second part explains the concepts of Xtext. The third part illustrates the result of the Xtext evaluation. Finally, the fourth part concludes this report.

# 2. MDSD and the MDA standard

"[MDSD] is the generic term for techniques creating runnable software from formal models automatically." ([1], p. 11) In opposite to model-based development where the model serves as documentation only in MDSD the model takes the role of the code so that there is no gap between documentation and implementation (from [1], p. 3). This is only possible if the model is formal. Formal means that a model is described that precisely that it can be processed by software (from [3]).

MDA is a subset of MDSD (from [1], p. 36). In opposite to MDSD, MDA is a standard defined by the Object Management Group (OMG) (from [3]). Its definition is still in progress (from [1], pp. 4-5). While MDSD focuses on effectively usable components in general, MDA specifies the technologies to be used to guarantee interoperability between utilities: MOF and UML (from [3], [1], pp. 4-5).

MDA differs between Platform Independent Models (PIM) and Platform Specific Models (PSM) (from [1], p. 36). It recommends the usage of multi-level transformations (from [1], p. 36). This approach offers multiple possibilities to customize the transformation process but also results in a higher development effort of the utility. In contrast single-level transformations are easier to develop but there has to be a special focus on the independence of the model from the platform.

In opposite to so-called General Purpose Languages (GPL) as Java, Domain Specific Languages (DSL) are programming languages of a domain and used to describe formal models (from [1], p. 30). They can be categorized under different aspects as follows: Internal DSLs are embedded in a GPL which is the host language (from [1], p. 98, [5]). In contrast, external DSLs are not bound to the limitations of a host language (from [1], p. 98, [5]). A vertical DSL or business DSL is a language which is used by non-IT staff in general to describe models of a business domain which are usually non-technical (from [5]). In opposite to a vertical DSL a horizontal DSL is used by developers to describe a whole application (from [5]). Furthermore DSLs can be textual or graphical (e.g. UML is a graphical DSL, CSS is a textual DSL in the broadest sense but not part of MDSD). A DSL consists of a concrete and an abstract syntax or rather the metamodel. The concrete syntax defines the textual or graphical form to describe DSL elements. The abstract syntax describes the data structures the object net is created with.

Formal models describe a domain with more abstract elements than available in a GPL as well as more specific elements than possible in a GPL because each element has a domain specific meaning which is its semantics (from [1], pp. 13-14). There is a static and a dynamic semantics. In opposite to the dynamic semantics the static semantics always can be described formally (from [1], p. 30) e.g. in terms of constraint checks. The dynamic semantics can be described formally or exists intuitively (from [1], p. 30). However finally, it is the interpretation of a generator or interpreter.

Formal models can be transformed into each other (Model To Model Transformation, M2M) and into code (Model To Text Transformation, M2T) (from [1], pp. 14-16). MDSD splits the complexity in two parts: The model with the reduced complexity – due to abstraction – and the (generated) code of the target platform with the actual complexity (from [1]. pp. 13-14).

Also after extensive changes a MDSD software product's architecture stays homogeneous because of the equal and central changeable generation process for all model elements of one type (from [1], p. 14).

A M2T generator generates code for a specific platform. The platform consists of the existing Application Programming Interfaces (API) which are part of the so called not generated artifacts as well as the generated artifacts and the manually implemented code (from [1], p. 34). In theory it is possible to write multiple generators for different platforms but in practice this is difficult because the semantics of a model often is influenced by the platform the first software product is developed for. Thus development of a generator for another platform with the same semantics can be very expensive (from [1], p. 15).

Once a DSL and its generators are matured through the development of one or more software products they can be reused efficiently in other projects of that kind. Only in this case the development velocity with these DSLs and generators can be higher than in projects with fully manual implementation (from [1], p. 15) because the developers are free of error-prone and tiresome routine work (from [1], p. 13). Additionally the expertise of the DSL and generator developers is included in the automated process and thus can be reused by other project members (from [1], p. 15).

Indeed MDSD offers a potentially high software quality but no guaranty (from [1], p. 16, [2], p. 155). To ensure a MDSD product's quality, besides the language and the generators also the models created with that language have to be tested. It is also possible to generate Tests partially. It is not recommended to generate the full test suite because this can result in successfully running tests and defective software products comparably which destroy a team's motivation (from [1], p. 253).

# 3. Xtext

Xtext is a Language Development Framework developed by the Itemis AG (from [6], p. 47). It is part of the Eclipse Modeling Project and open source[10] (from [7]). Xtext can be used to develop textual external DSLs as well as full-blown GPLs (from [6], p. 46). Currently it is available in version 2.2.1.

A Xtext grammar is represented by a file with the extension "xtext". It defines grammar rules in an Extended Backus-Naur-Form (EBNF)-like syntax (from [6], p. 56). In addition, a grammar rule defines a concrete syntax with the metamodel types that are instantiated in the Abstract Syntax Tree (AST) as well as their interfaces (from [6], pp. 68). A grammar can use existing metamodels or declare the generation of the derived metamodel (from [6], pp. 51). A Xtext grammar can also extend multiple other grammars. This is called "Grammar Mixin" ([6], p. 55).

Additionally, Xtext derives parser, linker, serializer and a full-blown Integrated Development Environment (IDE) or rather Eclipse editor plugin from a grammar. Therefore the Xtext project wizard creates three projects for one language by default: The language and generator project itself containing the grammar, an empty test project and the IDE project. Thus the grammar file always is the main documentation of a Xtext DSL (from [6], pp. 49).

The generation of a Xtext project's artifacts is freely configurable with a MWE2 work flow file (from [6], pp. 163). Xtext generators can be developed for both multi-level and single-level transformations. Xtext offers a large API to derive, interpret and generate Java classes from a model directly (from [6], pp. 131-139) in a single-level transformation (M2T). By default generation is always triggered after a model file is saved.

Because of the compact project structure and its simple central language declaration Xtext is suitable for agile software development with short cycles (see also [8]).

Xtext parsers are generated with the ANTLR Parser Generator. Thus Xtext also supports features like syntactic predicates to disambiguate ambiguous grammars (from [6], pp. 66).

---

[10] Xtext is published under Eclipse Public License (EPL)

## 3.1 Dependency Injection with Google Guice

Xtext component implementations are injected using Google Guice following the principle of Dependency Injection (from [6], pp. 77). Every attribute in a Java class that references another component can be annotated with the @Inject annotation (from [6], pp. 77). A class with the suffix "RuntimeModule" is contained in a Xtext project and binds implementations to interfaces for injection in the annotated attributes of all other classes in the project. In a RuntimeModule an implementation is bound to an interface if there is a method with the short name of the bound interface with the prefix "bind" returning the Class object of the implementation. Hence it is possible to customize almost every implementation that is bound with this annotation in a Xtext project.

## 3.2 Separation of manually implemented and generated code

Generated and manually implemented code should not be mixed[11] but clearly separated from each other so that it is not necessary to check generated code into a repository and to keep a project clear (from [12]).

Xtext separates generated code from manually implemented code clearly. A Xtext project contains a src folder for manual implementations only and a src-gen folder for generated code only[12]. In terms of the Generation Gap Pattern, manually implemented classes extend generated classes (see also [9]). Generated Java classes – the generated artifacts – extend base classes – the not generated artifacts or rather the generated artifacts of an extended Xtext language project. By default a generator of a Xtext language IDE also writes into a src-gen folder. It is configurable in the project properties. In addition, the Xtext API supports multiple output folders under different names that can be referenced in a generator.

---

[11] Some generators support so called protected regions to mark areas inside a generated file that are manually implemented.

[12] Xtend projects also contain a xtend-gen folder for generated Java classes.

## 3.3 Ecore as metamodel

The open source[13] technology Ecore is the metamodel of the Eclipse Modeling Framework (EMF) which is a main part of the Eclipse Modeling Project (from [4], pp. 3-17). In Xtext the Ecore metamodel is used to define the abstract syntax and an Ecore generator model for the generation of the appropriate runtime API to construct the AST in the DSL's parser (from [6], p. 205). Ecore models have the "ecore" extension. The structure of a Ecore model is similar to that of an UML class diagram. An Ecore model can contain elements of type EPackage, EClass, EDataType, EAttribute and EReference as shown in figure 1 (from [4], pp. 17).

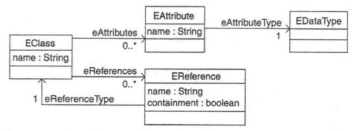

Figure 1: Simplified subset of the Ecore metamodel ([4], p. 17)

A Xtext language's model file in Eclipse is represented by an Ecore Resource instance containing the described object net. A ResourceSet instance contains every Resource object in the workspace (from [4], p. 31-34). Since contained Ecore references (EReference) are always bidirectionally navigable, a DSL created with Xtext can contain cross references to any other Ecore model element instance contained in any other Resource in the workspace. Figure 2 shows the component structure of a Xtext project focusing on its model's interfaces and compatibility of Xtext to other EMF-based utilities. Since Ecore is the common metamodel of the Eclipse Modeling Project or rather any EMF-based utility (from [4], p. 17)[14] and "Ecore has its roots in MOF and UML" (from [4], p. 131) its usage is conform with the MDA concept.

---

[13] Published under Eclipse Public License (EPL).

[14] There is also an EMF-based UML2 plugin.

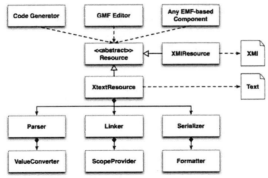

Figure 2: Components and model interfaces of a
Xtext project ([6], p. 206)

## 3.4 Definition of Syntax and Semantics

Xtext can derive the abstract syntax from the concrete syntax defined with the
grammar language. The example grammar MyDsl shown in figure 3[15] describes a simple fictional vertical DSL to define persons and their knowledge
about each other as reference. The "generate" keyword declares the Ecore
EPackage that is derived when generating the language by running the grammar file as "Generate Xtext Artifacts" in Eclipse. A grammar does not have to
generate an EPackage. A Xtext grammar rule can also specify the concrete
syntax for an existing abstract syntax. If a grammar does not contain any rules
a new EPackage has to be derived from the "generate" declaration can be left
(from [6], pp. 51),

Figure 3: Concrete (left) and derived abstract syntax described by an Ecore
metamodel (middle) and visualized with an Ecore Diagram (right)

Finally, an IQualifiedNameProvider has to be implemented to run the example. It defines the qualified name under which a person instance can be referenced. Therefore the id attribute is used. By default Xtext includes all available instances of an Ecore type in the scope of a reference of the same type so

---

[15] Ecore Diagram is part of the Ecore Tools SDK which is not included in the EMF plugin.

that in this case nothing more has to be implemented. The running IDE of the example language of figure 3 is shown in figure 4.

Figure 4: The running example language IDE

The example of figure 4 already shows that there are constraints that have to be checked. E.g. Max Mustermann may not reference himself because this semantic exists implicitly. In such cases a custom scope provider or validator implementation is required. A scope contains the elements that can be linked by the linker. A validator checks constraints after the AST is constructed. In general both loose scoping and strong validation are recommended because if scoping is too strong the modeler knows if he made a mistake but he doesn't know any details. In opposite to a scope provider a validator can return detailed custom warnings or error messages to the modeler but it is only able to validate what has already been linked.

The example has shown how easy it is to declare a Xtext grammar and implement the semantics.

## 3.5 Xbase

Xtext already contains a language implementation called Xbase. It concerns a statically typed GPL similar to Java (from [6], pp. 139). Thus it is possible to integrate Java expressions in any own Xtext language by extending Xbase. Xbase has a very slim concrete syntax. E.g. it is not necessary to declare the type of a variable if it is derivable from an assignment. Additionally, Xbase supports a short syntax to access properties by getter and setter as well as closures, operator overloading and so-called Extension Methods to call on objects that did not declare them by themselves (from [6], pp. 148-162). Xbase does not differ between expressions and statements: Everything is an expression (from [6], p. 147). Hence Xbase code is quickly-writable and can be very clear.

Xbase uses a metamodel of the Java Virtual Machine (JVM) and defines a concrete syntax (Xtype) (from [6], p. 139-146) to cross-reference as well as a name convention for parser rules to import JVM types (from [6], p. 22). A JVM type can be derived from any object of a custom language's AST (from [6], pp. 136). Xbase' default generator implementation generates each Java class that has been derived from a model element. Xbase's expressions can also be interpreted. Hence by deriving a JVM model both constraints of the Java platform are checked and plain Java classes are generated or expressions interpreted. This increases the development velocity. Java is the target platform of Xbase (from [6], p. 140) and thus any extending language.

Using Xbase without extending it, for one file with the extension "xbase" a Java class with the same name is generated. Figure 5 shows a Xbase file using a closure and an Extension Method from the Xtend library. It prints "[2, 3]" on execution of the generated Java class.

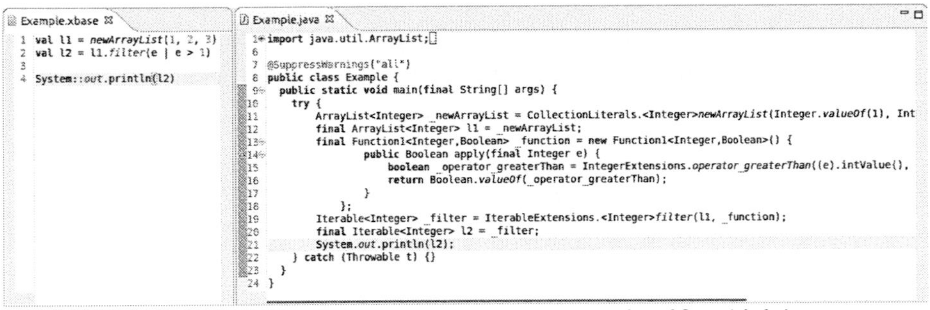

Figure 5: Example of a Xbase file (left) and its generated artifact (right)

## 3.6 Xtend

Xtend is a statically typed GPL (from [6], p. 176) extending Xbase (from [10]). A Xtend file represents a Java class (from [6], pp. 176). Xtend can also be separately installed in Eclipse. In Xtext Xtend is primarily used for manual extension of language or generator components. So-called dispatch functions, Extension Methods and Rich Strings are some of Xtend's main advantages (from [6], p. 176).

The "dispatch" keyword can be used to make multiple methods with different argument types of the same inheritance hierarchy polymorphic (from [6], pp. 181). To realize that the Xtend generator generates a group of dispatch methods with an underscore as name prefix and one method that decides which method to call depending on its argument's type at runtime. Thus it is not necessary to implement the Visitor Pattern (from [6], p. 181).

To add the scope of a Xtend class' attribute to the class itself the attribute can be marked with the "extension" keyword (from [6], p. 179). Additionally, all methods of the class' scope can be called on every object being conform with the method first argument's type (from [6], p. 179). Usually Google Guice is used to inject such extensions. Extension Method usage is orange-colored in the IDE editor like shown in figure 6.

Xtend also supports so-called Rich Strings that can occupy multiple lines and contain strings as well as control flow statements or rather expressions (from [6], p. 199-201). Their syntax is a subset of Xtend's predecessor language Xpand (from [10]). Rich Strings are generated as StringBuilder code and therefore come with high-performance. Rich Strings are also characterized by their clarity in particular. The Java generator generates indents relative to the indentation of the Rich String in the code ignoring lines with control flow statements. This behavior is marked in the IDE with a gray background as shown in figure 6. Hence both generator code and generated code are well-readable. Additionally, no separate concept for generator templates is required: Templates can be organized in an object orientated way.

```
class MyGenerator {

    def toClass(Entity e) '''
        public class «e.name» {
            «FOR p : e.properties»
                «p.toJavaProperty»
            «ENDFOR»
        }
    '''

    def toJavaProperty(Property p) {
        // ...
    }
}
```

Figure 6: Rich String and Extension Method in Xtend

# 4. Evaluation of horizontal DSL development with Xtext

As evaluation of the development velocity and learning curve of Xtext three textual horizontal DSLs extending Xbase have been developed within three month[16]. The appropriate IDE plugins enable developers to model and generate runnable Create-Read-Update-Delete (CRUD) Java Enterprise Edition web applications. The generators use "platform idioms" ([1], p. 34) which are Best Practices of the platform to efficiently generate code.

---

[16] Consult my bachelor thesis „Evaluierung der Modellgetriebenen Softwareentwicklung mit Xtext" for more details.

76

# 4.1 The DSL implementations

The QueryLanguage allows modeling of type-safe dynamic queries and generation of Java Persistence API (JPA) Criteria API code. With the ModelLanguage entities with Data Access Objects (DAO) containing queries defined with the QueryLanguage and referencing controller can be described and generated as annotated JPA entities and Enterprise Java Beans (EJB). Therefore the ModelLanguage extends the QueryLanguage. With the ViewLanguage view structures can be declared and data bound as well as methods invoked. ViewLanguage models are generated as Java Server Faces (JSF) Composite Components, Compositions, so-called ViewModels containing the parameters of a view and session-scoped ManagedBeans using (also generated) EJBs (from the ModelLanguage). Thus the code generation is split into multiple folders: While ManagedBeans are generated in the default output folder src-gen, Composite Components are generated in the src-view-gen folder. There is another generator output folder called resource. Every generated file inside is generated once and won't be overwritten or deleted so that the modeler can modify or add files arbitrarily. This folder is required to generate default and manually changeable artifacts like the web.xml and the application's JSF template and its CSS file.

Because of the derivation of the JVM model representation of each grammar element JVM model elements are referenced only and checked for specific interfaces. Thus it is also possible to use existing or manual implemented Java classes in a model. In such cases a special documentation of what is platform independent and what is not is required.

All types of Xtext and EMF components that have been implemented manually during development of the above language projects are listed below with a short explanation:

- **IQualifiedNameProvider:** Provides segmented qualified names for referenceable DSL objects of specific types. (e.g. de.myCompany.myApp.MyType)

- **IValueConverterService:** Converts a DSL value to a Java object. (e.g. convert "1.2" to Double)

- **IJvmModelInferrer:** Derives JVM model objects from DSL objects.

- **IScopeProvider:** Defines the scope of a DSL reference (EReference).

- **ITypeProvider:** Defines the JVM type of an instance of a XExpression which is Xbase's expression type or the JVM model interface JvmIdentifiableElement which is the super type of all JVM model elements. It performs the statically typing of every Xbase or JVM model object.

The default implementation XbaseTypeProvider should be extended if the abstract syntax is enhanced implementing the XExpression or JvmIdentifiableElement interface.

- **EValidator:** Validates the AST and creates errors or warnings when broken constraints indicated.

- **IFormatter:** Defines rules to format DSL code. A Xtext DSL's IDE uses the rules to format the selected model file's content when pressing Ctrl+Shift+F.

- **XbaseCompiler:** Compiles XExpression objects to Java code. XbaseCompiler is the default implementation for the compilation of XExpressions. It should be extended when adding a new abstract syntax to Xbase's XExpression.

- **IGenerator:** Generates the derived JVM model of a custom DSL's model. Xbase's JvmModelGenerator is the default implementation and generates plain Java classes from every JVM model object derived by the IJvmModelInferrer implementation. (E.g. in the ModelLanguage platform-specific annotations are added to the derived JVM model before executing the default code generation with the JvmModelGenerator simply)

- **IOutputConfigurationProvider:** Configures available output folders and maps them to identifiers.[17]

Using Google Guice each implementation of such a component has to be bound in the language project's RuntimeModule. Besides the grammar file in general the implementations of the component interfaces listed above completely specify a Xtext DSL. Smaller DSLs may require less or none manual implementations of these components.

## 4.2 The Reference Model

Below the reference model extracts of every developed DSL are illustrated within the following figures to visualize the power of Xtext. The reference model is an example model representing the real semantic meaning of every used element of the DSL it is modeled with (from [1], p. 222). It can be reproduced by executing the product which consists of the generated and not generated artifacts and the optionally manual implementations. This reference model describes an application used to edit customers and register associated incoming and outgoing letters for service in a middle-class office. The ModelLanguage model shown in figure 7 describes the required entities.

---

[17] Only manual implementation of any developed DSL's IDE shown here.

```
mailbookEntities.model ⊠
 1  package de.algorythm.mailbook.model {
 2      import de.algorythm.modelingUtils.rt.architecture.Pagination
 3      import java.util.List
 4
 5⊕     entity Customer {⬚
11
12⊕     embeddable Contact {⬚
17
18⊖     entity Letter {
19          date : TDate
20          incoming : TBoolean
21          customer : * ref Customer opposite letters
22
23⊖         dao {
24⊖             def listAllPaginated(c : Customer) : Pagination<Letter> {
25                  SELECT PAGINATED l FROM Letter l WHERE l.customer = [c]
26              }
27
28⊖             def listAll(c : Customer) : List<Letter> {⬚
31          }
32      }
33  }
```

Figure 7: Reference model mailbookEntities.model in Eclipse

Figure 8 shows an extract of another ModelLanguage model defining the required controller by cross-referencing derived JVM types of the mailbookEntities.model.

```
controller ApplicationController {
    inject customerDAO : CustomerDAO
    inject letterDAO : LetterDAO

    def listCustomersPaginated() : Pagination<Customer> {
        customerDAO.listAllPaginated
    }

    def createCustomer() : Customer {
        EntityFactory::createCustomer
    }
```

Figure 8: Extract of the reference model
mailbookController.model in Eclipse

An extract of the ViewLanguage model defining three views to manage customers and letters is shown in figure 9. The LetterListFragment represents the list of letters. It can not be triggered outside any view but embedded in other views.

```
mailbookView.view ✕                                                    ▭ ❑
 1  package de.algorythm.mailbook.^view {
 2      import de.algorythm.mailbook.control.ApplicationController
 3      import de.algorythm.mailbook.model.entity.Customer
 4      import de.algorythm.mailbook.model.entity.Letter
 5      import de.algorythm.modelingUtils.rt.architecture.Pagination
 6      import java.util.List
 7
 8      category Customers {
 9
10          view CustomerList() {▯
56
57          view CustomerEdit(c : Customer) {▯
79      }
80
81      category Letters {▯
122
123     fragment LetterListFragment(letters : Pagination<Letter>) {
124         data {
125             ctrl controller : ApplicationController
126         }
127
128         pagination letters
129         table l : letters.current {
130             col title = output "ID" output l.id.toString
131             col title = output "Date" output l.date.toString
132             col title = output "Incoming" output if (l.incoming) "yes" else "no"
133             col title = output "Customer" output l.customer.name
134             col title = output "Options" {
135                 button "delete" action = {controller.deleteLetter(l) letters.refresh null}
136             }
137         }
138         pagination letters
139     }
140 }
```

Figure 9: Extract of the reference model mailbookView.view in Eclipse

It becomes apparent that the language's syntax is not yet matured. It should be revised in a few more iterations. Additionally, required parts of the generator and the not generated artifacts are not yet implemented. Thus the model contains several workarounds to be able to run the application.

Figures 10, 11 and 12 show the execution of the modeled application. Obviously, the model contains several semantic mistakes: There is no button to create a new Contact object, a letter can be added without an associated customer and the check boxes corresponding to the "delete all selected" button in figure 11 are missing. These are simple examples how MDSD does not guarantee software quality.

However, in general the DSLs and generators work as the runnable mail book application proves.

Thus developing textual horizontal DSLs with Xtext is also possible without much effort. But the generator implementation has to be handled with care: It has to be separated from the language under both associative and semantic aspects. That means on the one hand that the language is not allowed to reference generator implementations directly to be able to change the generator implementation. However, on the other hand it has to be considered that a model's semantics is always influenced by the platform (e.g. persistence behavior of the ModelLanguage is influenced by JPA).

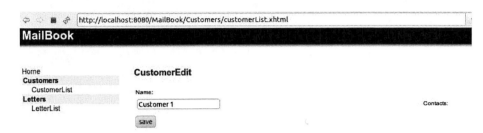

Figure 10: Editing a Customer object in the CustomerEdit view

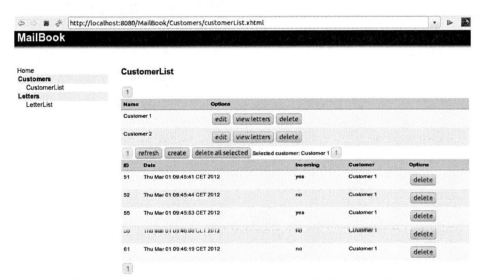

Figure 11: Listing customers and associated letters in the CustomerList view

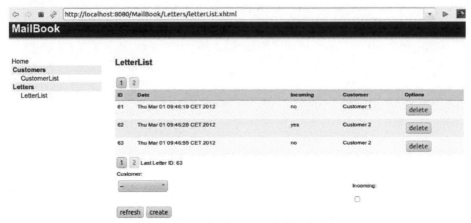

Figure 12: Listing and adding letters in the LetterList view

# 5. Conclusion

Xtext implements a lot of MDSD's Best Practices like the separation of manually implemented and generated code, the integration of the generator in the build process and the possibility to use the resources of the target platform within the model (see also [12]).

Since Xtext offers possibilities to use and generate metamodels as well as multiple inheritance of grammars, it is possible to separate and combine sub-domains and their DSLs.

Due to Xtext's compatibility with other EMF-based utilities it is conform with the MDA concept even though Xtext is not part of the standard.

Xbase closes the gap between documentation and code completely: It allows the definition of imperative expressions within own DSLs aiming Java code generation with ease.

However, the code generation of other target languages than Java from Xbase is not intended.

Due to the equal code generation process for every DSL object of the same type the generated software architecture is homogeneous.

Since Xtext offers a very steep learning curve, a high development velocity and central customization possibilities, it lends itself to agile development with short cycles.

The Xtend language is very suitable for both generator development and rapid development of every other purpose on the Java platform. It increases the manual implementation velocity.

It is very easy to develop Xtext DSLs but it takes a long time until a DSL and its generator are matured. Parallel development of models and appropriate DSLs is recommended. Thus at least at the beginning MDSD requires higher costs. Additionally, full independence of a model to a platform takes a lot effort. Hence MDSD should be practiced if one of the conditions listed below applies to a software project (cf. 13-16):

- Development of multiple software products of the same family.

- Development of long-term software products with changing architectures.

- Requirement that the user has to be able to express himself in domain-specific terms (business DSL).

# References

[1]   T. Stahl, M. Völter, S. Efftinge, A. Haase, "Modellgetriebene Softwareentwicklung", dpunkt.verlag, 2nd edition 2007

[2]   R. Petrasch, O. Meimberg, "Model Driven Architecture", dpunkt.verlag, 1th edition 2006

[3]   S. Frankel, J. Parodi, "The MDA Journal: Model Driven Architecture Straight from the Masters", Meghan-Kiffer Press, 1st edition 2004, pp. 17

[4]   D. Steinberg, F. Budinsky, M. Paternostro, Ed Merks, EMF: Eclipse Modeling Framework, Pearson Education Inc., 2nd edition 2009

[5]   Warmer IT, Domain Specific Languages, Retrieved February 29, 2012 from http://www.openmodeling.nl/dsl

[6]   Eclipse Foundation, Xtext 2.1 Documentation, Retrieved February 19, 2012 from http://www.eclipse.org/Xtext/documentation/2_1_0/Xtext%202.1%20Documentation.pdf

[7]   Itemis AG, Xtext, Retrieved February 22, 2012 from http://xtext.itemis. com

[8]   Itemis AG, Xtext – Eclipse Modeling – Services und Lösungen – Xtext AG, Retrieved March 16, 2012 from http://www.itemis.de/itemis-ag/services-und-loesungen/eclipse-modeling/language=de/27262/xtext

[9]   IBM, Generation Gap, Retrieved February 28, 2012 from
      http://www.research. ibm.com/designpatterns/pubs/gg.html, 28.02.2012

[10]  Sven Efftinge, Sven Efftinge's Blog: Xtend2 – the Successor to Xpand,
      Retrieved February 29, 2012 from http://blog.efftinge.de/2010/12/
      xtend-2-successor-to-xpand.html

[11]  Itemis AG, About Xtext – xtext, Retrieved February 22, 2012 from
      http://xtext.itemis. com/xtext/language=en/36527/about-xtext

[12]  Sven Efftinge, InfoQ: Best Practices for Model-Driven Software Devel-
      opment, Retrieved March 16, 2012 from
      http://www.infoq.com/articles/model-driven-dev-best-practices